The World in My Mind,
My Mind in the World

The World in My Mind, My Mind in the World

Igor Aleksander

imprint-academic.com

Published in the UK by Imprint Academic
PO Box 200, Exeter EX5 5YX, UK

Published in the USA by Imprint Academic
Philosophy Documentation Center
PO Box 7147, Charlottesville, VA 22906-7147, USA

ISBN 1 84540 021 6 (cloth, 2005)
ISBN13: 9 781845 401023 (pbk., 2007)

A CIP catalogue record for this book is available from the
British Library and US Library of Congress

Contents

Preface

About this Book: Why the world in my mind?

There is no shortage of books on consciousness, so why write another one? Over the last five years since I finished my last book[1] something has become blindingly clear to me. Consciousness is many things: at least, as we shall see, I have identified five that seem crucial. A scan of the many of the excellent books that claim to explain consciousness does not reveal systematic attempts at breaking consciousness down into simpler elements to make the concept more accessible. This is like trying to explain how a grandfather clock works without referring to the pendulum and weights. I first published this five-step idea as a journal article[2] based on a contribution to a small, fascinating meeting at the Cold Spring Harbour Laboratories in 2001 (http://www.swartzneuro.org/banbury_e.asp) organised by Christof Koch , David Chalmers and Rod Goodman. The question was 'Can a Machine Be Conscious?' and there was a surprising degree of agreement that one could — a notion that has driven my research since the late 1980s. But looking at the arguments put forward by myself and others made me realise that the level of technical detail we use to make our respective cases is dire. This prevents communication not only among the experts but certainly between the experts and anyone out there who

---

[1] Aleksander, I. (2000), *How to Build a Mind: Dreams and Diaries* (London: Weidenfeld and Nicolson; paperback ed. Phoenix 2001).
[2] Aleksander, I. & Dunmall, B. (2003), 'Axioms and tests for the presence of minimal consciousness in agents', *Journal of Consciousness Studies*, **10** (4–5), 7–19.

would like to know more about consciousness and join in the debate.

Koch talks about the neural correlates of consciousness and coalescence, Chalmers of something called the logical non-supervenience of consciousness on the physical brain and Goodman with others argues that model-referenced control systems are the answer. I talk of five formally stated axioms. This, therefore, is why I have written this book. All this specialist mumbo jumbo does map into normal language. And once fixed in normal language it may be used to answer questions that many of us have about the nature, origin and use of consciousness.

I start with five *axioms* — there we go, why use a word such as 'axiom'? What is it? An axiom is a plausible idea, rather than a proven truth, on which one can build sensible explanations of things. So being conscious for me breaks down into five basic ideas that raise important questions to which I try to provide plausible answers. Here are the five axioms or steps of this book and the questions that they prompt. The book is about the answers.

- The major part of being conscious is my sensation **of being an entity in an out-there world**. How does this happen?

- Another part of being conscious is that **I am an entity in time**: I have a remembered past and I can take a few guesses about the future. What mechanisms have this property?

- It is remarkable that we have similar brain mechanisms but they lead to different personalities and different ways of being conscious. Something called '**attention**' is at work here: what is it and how does it work?

- My mind seems constantly engaged in sifting choices about **what to do next**. How does it do this to my best advantage?

- I seem to be influenced and guided by things I call **emotions**. What are they?

Since the mid 1990s, I also have written about the way in which machines could be conscious.[3] I came to the conclusion that, more than a non-human animal, a conscious machine could come close to discussing its own consciousness. This does not mean that machines will compete with us in late night conversations of whether this or that philosopher is right. It does mean, however, that, having got close to the mechanisms of consciousness through the design of machines, helps to answer the axiomatic questions I raised earlier. So the ideas in this book are driven by two strong impulses. The first is that I need to be outrageously introspective. I shall talk of those strange things that I feel personally as indicators of what needs to be explained. The second is that explanations should be cast in terms of simple principles that anyone can understand. I don't want to give the impression that I am the first to have given thought to this type of deliberation. Indeed, some of the book discusses the fascinating and diverse thoughts of others, but my personal experience and what mechanisms might be involved are the twin schemes through which the five steps to being conscious are taken.

The first chapter (**Capturing the Butterfly of Thought**), owes its title from an early task we set our models of conscious mechanisms: to imagine a butterfly. This got quite a lot of undue publicity along the lines of being a 'break-through' in building the world's first conscious machine. Nothing could have been further from the truth: the machine called Magnus *was not* conscious but was the first dedicated piece of software that enabled us to study hypotheses about the way that consciousness might emerge from brain structure.

This chapter asks what is to be gained by building machines and how does this help those who do not generally build things? First, building things requires a clear definition of what will be built. Words like *thought*, *consciousness* and *mind* are given an operational character. Second, it establishes that 'being conscious' is about *mechanisms* that make us conscious which is a saner way to go than wondering about *'having consciousness'*

[3]   Aleksander, I. (1996), *Impossible Minds: My Neurons, My Consciousness* (London: Imperial College Press).

which promulgates the mistaken idea that consciousness is a property like having a leg or a cold. The work and ideas of others who build things are also discussed.

How do we decide that one thing is conscious and another is not? In the second chapter (**The Five Tests for Being Conscious**), I side with those who say that it is virtually impossible to tell if an organism is conscious just by observing the thing behave. But digging deep into ourselves we know what major sensations would seriously affect our being conscious were they to be missing. This is where the five axioms come from and this is the chapter in which they get a thorough airing. These then become the targets for identifying which parts of the brain are involved in the axiomatic phenomena and what kind of computational machinery could possibly do the same thing. Luckily it is not necessary to have a PhD in computer design to understand the arguments that are involved in looking at being conscious from the point of view of 'how could a machine do it?'. This is precisely where the notion of 'capturing the butterfly of thought' comes in. I think of a butterfly but wonder what it is in the activity my brain cells that makes it into a butterfly. If the cells of a machine can do the same thing, have a sense of self, attend to important things in its world, plan and evaluate its plans, we will be well on the way to being much clearer about what it is to be conscious.

An exceedingly strange thing that my brain does is to deprive me of the power of thought about once a day, usually at night. Chapter 3 (**Sleep, Dreams and the Unconscious**) is about the relationship between what we call being conscious, its loss when sleeping, its peculiar reappearance when dreaming and its disappearance while being anaesthetised. We also hear stories about something called 'the unconscious'. It may seem odd that having hardly got into what it is to be conscious I slip into discussing what it might be to be unconscious. Perhaps this is not so strange given that understanding the difference between the two makes *being* conscious stand out from *not being* conscious. What is sleep for? What is the difference between what goes on when I am awake, when I sleep and when I dream? After all during the latter my brain is fully alive and working. Here we begin to flex the muscles of the axioms of chapter 2 to give us some insights into these areas of our existence in which the 'self' appears to have taken a holiday. We look at what is known from brain-wave measurements and then take a look at a little simulation that throws light on what sleep experts call the 'sleep cycle'. Axioms are also helpful in clarifying what Freud might have meant by 'the unconscious'.

In Chapter 4 (**The Octopus with a Stomach Ache**) I wonder whether non-human animals are conscious. Experiments on the octopus show a remarkable ability to plan and assess long sequences of events. This is just one example of what makes the question of animal consciousness of one of the most passionate debates in the science of consciousness. I look at the struggles of scientists who are designing experiments to discover glimmers of consciousness in animals. They surely are up against it. It is difficult enough to infer consciousness in people one knows well: the problem is immensely difficult when it comes to animals. But while the experiments mostly do not provide foolproof evidence of thinking as we know it, they virtually never cut some form of deliberative mental state out. In terms of the axioms of this book, theory has it that it is likely that animals are conscious — not of exactly the same things as we are, but conscious of what is important to *them* nonetheless. The axiomatic argument centers on the similarity of mechanisms between man and beast and the likelihood of such mechanisms doing similar things for both.

Can it happen that a gorilla can walk about in a crowd without being noticed? Yes it can as has been shown by a simple experiment that involves what psychologists call 'attention'. Those taking part in the experiment are asked to count the number of bounces of a ball in the film of a ball game played among a few young people. Only less than 20% notice a man in a gorilla suit when he crosses the playing field in a rather obvious way. Chapter 5 (**The Disappearing Gorilla**) examines this essential but peculiar behaviour of the brain. This kind of experiment leads some to believe that our feeling of being an entity in an out-there world is nothing but an illusion. I side with those who argue that the illusion idea is mistaken. Attention, which some call 'the gateway to consciousness' is a very useful device for selecting what gets into our consciousness out of a flood of sensory information. The process of selection is complex and sophisticated, forming the meat if this chapter. It is also what causes differences between us. No two people attend to the same things. This is why *some* people see the gorilla. Part of our personalities is determined by the way we attend to the world around us. But without attention we would drown in sensory information. So there can be situations in which the attention mechanism leaves things out. The axioms suggest that this is an exception and not a rule. Our vision is no illusion it is just not always perfect. This discussion also allows me to visit a theory recently put forward by Alva Noë of the University of California at Berkeley and Kevin O'Regan of the René Descartes University in Paris. They argue that the body, including the eyes, reacts to the world in an unconscious, automatic fashion. They see attention as the process of breaking into this process and thus becoming conscious. This would offend our axiom that deals with imagination (axiom2) as it is based on the idea that all the memory an organism needs is out there in the world. But then, how could we remember the past? I argue that a reconciliation of various points of view will make sense of that vital part of our consciousness: sensing the external world.

Illusions are fashionable in the modern philosophy of consciousness. In Chapter 6 (**Knowing What We Want**) I look at a philosophy that suggests that we kid ourselves when we think that we first want something and then go out to get it. This is based on an experiment carried out by Benjamin Libet which showed that participants asked to lift a finger had brain activity associated with this event *before* they became conscious of what they wanted. Who is pulling the strings? This impinges on issues of free will which have been central to our cultures for as long as one can say cultures existed. I take a look at some of the history of free will and then use some of the ideas of Chapter 2 to show first, that the illusion arguments leave out the brain activity due to the emotion which is involved when we make choices. When this is included, the illusion idea becomes less credible and reasons for our feeling of control over what we want are reinstated.

This book advocates strongly that there is a tight link between some neural activity in the brain and personal sensation. This appears to contradict the philosophy of David Chalmers, an influential contemporary consciousness philosopher who created the notion of the 'hard' problem of explaining sensation. That is, whatever you understand at a physical level does not bridge over to what you sense. In Chapter 7 (**Chalmers' Two Minds**) I take a close look at the hard problem and the explanatory gap between sensation and brain activity. Surprisingly, axiomatic arguments actually agree with the way Chalmers thinks that the gap might be bridged: through the use of informational and computational arguments.

Finally, in Chapter 8 (**Unfinished Business**), I suggest that this book is merely the beginning of what could be a level-headed way of removing a fear of mechanistic discussions of consciousness without losing the awe and respect that it commands. Here I briefly dip into some further important issues that are affected by the axiomatic arguments of this book. The idea of using computation to understand consciousness is under sustained attack. One of the most elegant assaults comes from geriatrician Ray Tallis and I look at the way that the axioms provide a defence.

Notable for its absence in the first seven chapters is the mention of natural language. Despite the very human (as opposed to 'animal') nature of this, I look at the way axiomatic mechanisms in humans might have this added facility over other animals. The ideas of Ludwig Wittgenstein and Noam Chomsky come into view while the axiomatic approach suggests structures that might resolve some questions that arise from these existing philosophies: consciousness of abstract ideas and whether language is inherited or acquired.

Probably the most important application of what is being said in this book is the provision of operational models for medicine as it relates to mental illness. Most mental illnesses are distortions of consciousness. For example, the memory problems of an Alzheimer's sufferer may be expressed as failures of imaginational machinery while something dire has gone wrong with the axiom 1 depictive machinery of a schizophrenic. I describe some work done with Helen Morton with Parkinson's sufferers. on visual planning deficits. Why should a lack of dopamine which normally affects movement interfere with working out how to move a few coloured spheres around? The axioms suggest an explanation.

Does the prospect of a mechanistic explanation of consciousness offend the religious beliefs of some? In this final part of the book I suggest that in the long term it should not not. It is merely another example of the way in which theology needs to be the philosophy for things that we do not fully understand, but must then give up this hold as science provides rational explanations. So as a moral of the story of this book, I suggest that the mechanistic steps we take, help us to appreciate the sophistication and subtlety with which the brain gives rise to our rich, exciting and highly effective inner life.

Appendix

This is included for those who want a brief technical introduction to the details of the kind of neural machinery which is used to create simulations of conscious systems. This culminates in a 'kernel' architecture that is used in various parts of the book.

Thanks

The ideas that fill this book do not occur as a result of monastic isolation. First I am grateful for the sustained discussions and email exchanges with my colleague Barry Dunmall. Despite being right in the thick of the laboratory work on conscious machines, he remained challengingly skeptical which certainly encouraged me to be clear about my assessments, assertions and axioms. I wish to thank my current doctoral students whose work in machine consciousness leads to progress: Kirk De Souza, Peter Liniker, Sunil Rao, Mercedes Lahnstein and Rabinder Lee. The title of this book owes its inspiration to Max Velmans who recently gave his professorial inaugural lecture entitled 'Is the World in the Brain or The Brain in the World?' His clarity of thought and thorough assessment of the philosophy of consciousness makes me feel happy to have been able to para-phrase the title of his lecture.

Thanks are due to the Leverhulme Trust whose help has made it possible to find time to write this book and to Imperial College for continuing to support my academic existence as an emeritus professor who finally can enjoy his research without worrying about external assessments and the extraction of funds from funding agencies.

Finally I thank Helen for continuing to show me how pleasur-able life is away from the computer screen, Joe and Melissa for being a smashing couple and bringing the delightful Luke and Tai into vivaciously conscious life, and Sam and Claudine for being another smashing couple who make the best *paõ de queso* in the world.

Chapter 1

Capturing the Butterfly of Thought

How machines may be used to understand consciousness

I am convinced that in principle it is possible to design machines that are conscious in much the same way as I am. I am also convinced that this is a direct and uncluttered way of understanding what it is to be conscious. The strategy for designing conscious machines is tough but, in the end, doable. It is founded on unravelling the undoubtedly complex functioning of the brain and transferring this understanding into computational machinery. Having done this, the 'virtual' brain in the computer can be subjected to the kind of fierce experimentation that could not be contemplated for real brains. The virtual brain then becomes a malleable vehicle with which to ask questions such as, under what conditions does it sustain being conscious and what is it to be unconscious but still functioning?

The key to what I propose will be explained in some depth in the next chapter while here it is possible to say that the strategy is rooted in five basic properties which feel inwardly to be important. These are the conjuring up of a 'self' in an 'out-there' world, the ability to imagine, the ability to attend to important events, planning ahead, and having feelings about what goes on and what might be done. The machines created in this way will not be conscious of the same things that I am conscious of, but if they are conscious of something, even if trivial and limited how they become conscious is available for study in a way that more sophisticated objects (like people or goats) is not. My machine might get somewhat concerned that its battery is running down, or that a human with whom she is interacting seems not to say things very clearly. What does it mean to say that *it is conscious* of the battery state and understanding a human instead of just being programmed to react to simple stimuli? This book sets out to answer this type of question.

But why bother with building machines? Yes, a conscious robot-driven car might be safer and cuddlier than an unconscious one, and a conscious robot on Mars might be happier to spend the rest of its life there than its human counterpart, but these are not the main reasons for thinking about conscious machines. As hinted a little earlier, designing conscious machines is a way of dissecting and understanding what it is to be conscious. Importantly you don't have to be an engineering genius to understand the principles of designing such machines. This chapter is the result of some of the ideas that have surfaced from having worked on the design of conscious machines since the mid 1990s and which can be shared with anyone who might be interested enough to listen.

But first there is a bit of background. Words in this area are treacherously slippery. I shall define what 'thought', 'mind' and 'being conscious' mean for me. In the philosophy of the last century there were important no-entry warning signs against a scientific assault on consciousness. William James and Thomas Nagel in very different ways have fired shots across the bows of foolhardy adventurers who set off down this road. I shall argue that their words have actually been helpful in shaping my enterprise.

Another foolhardy sin I propose to perpetrate is to rely heavily on introspection. This is somewhat of a break from the last 50 years of Artificial Intelligence where mimicking the outward behaviour of organisms thought to be intelligent has been the target. This too needs some elaboration. And then there is the butterfly — I have used it as a symbol of free thought. This featured rather too figuratively in the recent public history of building conscious machines as will be explained a little later.

Using mind words

As already said, matters of mind and brain are notorious for containing words that lack definition. All I can say is what *I* mean by them. This then will hopefully not change, at least within the confines of the covers of this book. For me, being conscious is all about being able to think. But what is it to think? Thought seems to have at least two major characteristics: perceptual and imaginative. The perceptual is the 'here and now'. You are now reading this book, I am (at a different 'now') sitting at a desk pushing the keys of my laptop writing it. In waking life, the perceptual is always there. It also has a special character. It puts me in the middle of a world which seems to exist thanks to my senses. Imaginative thought, on the other hand, can be in the past or the future. I easily remember who I am and where I have been. Failure to do this would be seen as a tragic abnormality, an unfortunate distortion of my ability to be conscious. Importantly, I can also think of where I want to be and what might happen if I take action to get me there. Thought involves emotion. If I feel angry or pleased, these emotions penetrate my thought and we shall see in the next chapter that emotions rather than being a failing of humans could be central to thought.

But what of 'mind'? I think of it as a kind of bucket that encompasses 'all that of which I am capable of thinking'. It has structure because there are certain thoughts that I will always think in a similar way. Sometimes these are called beliefs. I have ways of thinking that are distinct from others. I may not agree with others. 'I have changed my mind' or 'the answer to the question does not come to mind' are phrases that suggest that thoughts form a structure which, in the first case, needs to be modified and in the second, appears to be partly unreacheable.

Being conscious clearly involves the brain. I define 'being conscious' as the brain being in a state which supports thinking. Living brains do not always support thought: sleep, and anaesthesia are examples of the brain being fully active but not thinking. Dreaming, of course, is a funny thing that happens in sleep. More of this in Chapter 3. The way diseases and injury to the brain distort the conscious experience of the sufferers, for me underscores the fact that being conscious heavily depends on the physical state of the brain.

Avoiding 'consciousness' and being bats

I need to stress that, for me, the word 'consciousness' is fraught with difficulty and I sometimes wish that people did not use it at all. Ringing in my ears are the words of William James, the 'father of psychology' who lived in the early twentieth century:

> For twenty years I have mistrusted consciousness. It is the name of a non-entity and has no right place among first principles ...[1]

The way that the word 'consciousness' is often used is problematic because it implies that it is something we *have* in the way that we have two feet or a liver. This leads to one of the most poignant misunderstandings in scientific debates around this subject. It leads to the search for 'what consciousness is made of'. This could as silly as looking for what 'mobility' is made of in a mobile telephone. The question 'what makes a phone mobile?' is easily answered. So we must ask 'what makes me (or anything else) conscious?' and this leads us to look for an understanding of crucial brain mechanisms without confusing my 'being conscious' with a 'consciousness' that has no material form. William James spent a lifetime analysing what it is to 'be conscious' despite his pessimism about 'consciousness'.

William James would never have questioned that 'being conscious' was of enormous importance to living organisms. Being conscious is the centre of our living experience. We tend to take it for granted, until a mental disease distorts our thinking life. As said earlier being conscious is being in a state which supports 'thought' and 'thought' is the brain activity of creating an inner world in our heads that enables us and other living organism to examine what has passed, to be aware of what is in the present and, sensibly plan the future. In the case of humans it also allows

---

[1]   James, W. (1904), 'Does consciousness exist?', *Journal of Philosophy, Psychology and Scientific Methods*, **1**, 477–491.

us to build imagined worlds. Literature, theatre, cinema and the like, are a pleasure because of our ability to live in imagined worlds. But what is it to have pleasure, or fear or jealousy for that matter? Understanding this is on the agenda for the conscious machine builders: designing conscious machines is a way of explaining what being conscious is all about.

Thomas Nagel, a contemporary philosopher at New York University has had a huge influence in advocating that science can't reach an explanation of consciousness. He did this by asking the devastatingly simple question 'What is it like to be a bat?'[2] The implication is that because I cannot 'get into' being a bat, I cannot have a theory about what it is like to be one. The more shattering implication is that we cannot have a theory about any inner or *subjective* process because science is essentially an *objective* activity. However, Nagel's question is helpful as it allows me to explain that my quest is 'What does a bat need to have in its brain, to know what it's like to be a bat?' We easily believe that a rock does not know what it's like to be a rock because there is no evidence of it having any machinery that could have any knowledge at all. By the same argument the chess playing machine does not know what it's like to play chess as it has no machinery to do so — its machinery only plays chess. This line of argument leads to an answer to yet another question: 'What distinguishes a machine which is conscious from one that is not?'. Two machines could behave in the same way, but one could be driven by its own thought and the other by some programmer's idea of how a machine might behave. So, a direct way of arguing that a bat might be conscious is by being a bat-brain specialist and being able to say that the bat has all the necessary machinery in place for it to have a sense of self in an out-there world, an ability to imagine, and ability to attend, an ability to plan and an albeit embryonic ability to evaluate its plans through a process which in humans we call emotion. These are the five axiomatic tests for consciousness that I shall elaborate in the next chapter.

[2]   Nagel, T. (1974), 'What is it like to be a bat?', *Philosophical Review,* **83**, 435–450.

Introspection and not behaviour

Making things behave *as if* they are conscious tells us nothing about what it *is* to be conscious. So I stress that introspection, that is, looking inside myself to work out how things feel, is a more reliable guide to conscious machine design than behaviour. This distinguishes designing conscious machines from the work done for over the last 50 years under the heading of artificial intelligence or AI. The achievements of AI have been considerable. They dragged the computer out of being seen just as a super number cruncher to being able to solve logical problems which, if carried out by a human being, would be said to require intelligence. One of the achievements that is often quoted by the press as a triumph of AI is the defeat of Chess Master Boris Kasparov by the 'IBM Deep Blue' machine in 1997. The feat was achieved by a large number of programmers writing millions of program lines of the 'if X then Y' variety. The computer's competence lay entirely in the skill with which the programmers foresaw contingencies that could arise during the playing of the game and programmed them into the machine. So if 'outward behaviour' is the sole concern of the programmer, the system will have no sense of 'self', no ability to introspect. Detractors of the 'conscious machine' concept are fond of quoting this as an example of how no AI effort can lead to any form of consciousness in a computer. But this is due to just a limited way of thinking about computation. Starting with introspection as the key property of the machine design means that the involvement of the computer in a conscious machine is totally different from that which is done under the heading of AI. Where the AI researcher is interested in behaviour irrespective of mechanism, the conscious machine builder starts with as accurate a model of the object that is responsible for our being conscious: the human brain. So modelling rather than the simulation of behaviour becomes the alternative way of using the computer.

The art of modelling

In brain modelling the computer merely becomes an empty box within which the model of a brain is created. The computer is like the clay from which a model is moulded. And like clay, it is not the computer that captures the butterfly of thought but the model of the brain within it. In the language of computation this is called a 'virtual' brain, that is, something that can be studied like the brain, but is not the brain itself. Modelling is a commonplace technique for understanding complex systems in engineering, but a relatively new technique in understanding the brain. In engineering, a computer model is a way of finding out the value of a design before going to the expense of building the real thing. For example, in the design of a bridge, a virtual bridge may be tested for its excellence in terms of what it is to be a bridge. And what it is to be a bridge is the function of carrying loads across a gap. The virtual brain, hopefully, can be tested for its excellence in terms of what it is to be a brain. And the essence of what it is to be a brain is to be conscious. We leave aside for the moment the possible conceptual difference between 'being a bridge' and 'being conscious': this will be thrashed out in various parts of this book.

Of course it is impossible to model the brain in every detail: 11 billion cells grouped into about 100 interacting areas, the presence of chemical modulators, the complexity of sensory equipment such as the eyes just make a detailed model unattainable. For the conscious machine builder, modelling remains a delicate matter of simplifying the structure while still making sure that the function that needs to be studied or tested is not lost. Despite this, when things go right, the model can provide a tool for necessary experimentation which cannot be executed on real brains. In the case of the bridge, questions such as 'does it still hold its load if I remove these three struts?' can be asked. In the case of the brain the questions one would like to ask are something like: 'if I remove a particular little group of brain cells (neurons) will the brain remain conscious?'.

Some readers will see this as an outrageously difficult requirement. How does the model tell me whether the machine is conscious or not? This is the crux of what I have called 'capturing the butterfly of thought'. I shall try to explain this form of words by delving into the past of my own efforts of this kind of modelling.

Butterflies

We now live in an age when it is possible to discuss conscious machines without incurring too much flack from philosophers, neurologists or psychologists. Not so long ago, only consenting adults could avow to each other that such machines might be made. If the word got out, philosophical phrases of disapproval if not abuse would be attracted: 'dirty reductionists', 'unthinking functionalists' and so on. This was the ambience in 1996 when I lived through a rather embarrassing moment. It was a Sunday morning. The enduring 'Breakfeast with Frost' programme was on the television. The Sunday papers were being reviewed. The camera zoomed in on the front of the Sunday Times, and there it was: a colour picture of my face with a vast blue butterfly projected on it. Were this a parlour game I would now offer a bottle of champagne to the first person to guess the story behind this happening.

As there is no time for parlour games here is the story. A few days previously, I had been interviewed by one of that excellent crowd of British science journalists who, in bloodhound fashion, have a keen drive to find a scientific 'breakthrough' story. The interview was occasioned by two events, first I had just published the *Impossible Minds* book[3] and, second in the week to come I was to demonstrate a rather novel computer program in the Science Museum which we had built in my laboratory at Imperial College. It was called Magnus. This was a new simulation of the kind of circuits we have in our brain that had just sufficient detail to allow us to ask serious questions about some of the more puzzling things that brains do. The fact that being conscious seems to be entirely due to the brain, this is the most puzzling question of them all. We built Magnus as part of a quest to get to know more about how brains make us conscious. The way the newpaper put it was:

'Revealed: the computer that thinks it's alive'

There are undoubted dangers for hype and misunderstanding in this field. But why the butterfly? One take on the puzzle about

[3]   Aleksander, I. (1996), *Impossible Minds: My Consciousness, My Neurons* (London: Imperial College Press).

being conscious is that when I think of, say, a beautiful butterfly, one I had actually seen or one that I had just made up 'in my head', were a neurosurgeon to examine my brain with some super brain scanner, all she would notice is a small change in the 'firing' patterns of billions of tiny cells as my thoughts come and go. Projected on a screen, these firing patterns might look like fireworks or Christmas lights gone berserk. So, to put it rather too simply , the problem of trying to understand what in my brain makes me conscious, is precisely that of relating the neural fireworks to my inner thought. And, indeed, we had chosen to illustrate this property by making Magnus 'think' of a butterfly. Had there been any breakthrough, it was the fact that we had decoded the fireworks in the computer simulation to reveal the 'thought' on the screen.

'Firing' is the word used to describe what a brain cell (or 'neuron', to give it its usual name) does when it signals *to* other neurons that it has discovered something important in the messages it receives *from* other neurons. Firing in a brain neuron consists of a burst of electrical energy at the tip of the cell that takes the form of a rapid sequence of pulses — about 100 per second. By and large, neurons in the brain form networks that primarily respond with these firing patterns to incoming sensory information from eyes, ears etc. Not only do these networks react to the sensory input to our bodies, but they can also sustain some firing patterns just by being connected in intricate daisy-chains. Some of this inner activity is what we call imagination or contemplation.

So this was the demonstration that the reporter had witnessed. In our work we developed good reasons for thinking that if I say 'butterfly' to someone, their imagining neuron daisy chains will actually cause firing patterns that encode the remembered picture of a butterfly. So the speaking person would be able to say something like 'I am conscious of a butterfly in "my head"'. To put it ever so bluntly, the butterfly is hidden in the fireworks in much the same way that a picture of the head of a clown might be hidden in a 'join up the numbered dots' puzzle.

The blaze of TV lights

Like the front page of the Sunday Times, the walking into the lecture room for the demonstration at London's Science Museum also held an unpleasant surprise. The room was ablaze with lights for a battery of film crews. I fear that the enthusiastic publisher of my book *Impossible Minds* had issued a press release where he rather over-egged the notion that the world's first conscious machine was to be demonstrated. No amount of my explaining that the machine was designed to study what 'being conscious' *might be*, rather than to make the machine itself conscious, prevented headlines about conscious machines. Nor did it prevent a barrage of questions of the kind: 'Now that you have made a conscious machine, will it want to take over the world? Does it have to have rights?' I do not dismiss these questions for not being important. They are obviously part of a necessary debate which features in what I hope is a rational fashion in this book. But, at that moment, they did not apply to the Magnus machine as it was being demonstrated.

By decoding the simulated neural fireworks in Magnus back into the butterfly on the screen could be described in a rather eerie way as being able to see on a screen what Magnus was 'thinking'. This is relatively easy on computers because we can keep track of where the butterfly encoding neurons are, but it would be a nigh impossible task for a neurosurgeon and the living brain. The demonstration in the Science Museum was about how simple neural structures called neural 'automata' could perform several 'thought-like' acts: recognise visual patterns, remember visual patterns, use very simple word structures to describe their thinking and even dream in their own way. In addition to the explanation in *Impossible Minds* of how understanding 'automata' may be the right way of understanding what it is to be conscious, I have also had another look at these mechanisms and their history in *How to Build a Mind*, published in 2000.[4] I was convinced then as I am convinced now that the

---

[4]   Aleksander, I. (2000), *How to Build a Mind: Dreams and Diaries* (London: Weidenfeld and Nicolson; paperback ed. Phoenix 2001). The American edition (Columbia UP) was subtitled *Toward Machines with Imagination*.

mechanisms of consciousness are based in the properties of these neural automata. To describe the system that demonstrates such principles as *being* conscious was, however, premature.

In 1996, the claim that one could make conscious machines was and should have been treated with some suspicion. Major parts of a theory were missing. Why does some neural firing contribute to being conscious and some other does not? How does a 'self' arise? How does an organism use thought to plan into the future? What role does intention and attention play in being conscious? What are emotions and moods? What is the role of human language in the consciousness of humans? Many of these questions have now been clarified, and with very little hesitation I would say that there is no obstacle in the way of building a usefully conscious machine. Indeed some of the robots we have in our laboratories could be described as being conscious in some embryonic way. But these statements are not to lead to more headlines in Sunday papers. The hackneyed phrase 'Evolution not Revolution' is the way to approach being conscious through machine design.

Evolving to live with conscious machines.

A sign of evolution is that even hardened sceptics are beginning to accept that it will not be long before non-biological machines are built which are claimed to be conscious. It could even be that the machines themselves will claim that they are conscious. On the whole this is good news. It means that some of the mystical veils and taboos associated with the subject of consciousness are being lifted. Despite this, there are always those who believe that having a few mystical veils around may be necessary to keep up an interest in consciousness. But their numbers are dwindling. This does not mean that discussions about consciousness are becoming simply discussions about the cogs and gears of brains and brain-like machines. On the contrary, it becomes possible to discuss with greater freedom what is the object of consciousness. That is, why is it necessary for a bat or any other organism to be conscious, what exactly might a bat be conscious *of*, how does this differ from what I am conscious of, and what qualifies a mechanism to make it conscious?

The driving force of this evolution is that people with different views of consciousness are researching, meeting and thrashing out their differences. In the last few years, scientists and engineers, together with neurophysiologists, psychologists and philosophers have tried to develop some kind of a shared understanding of what it is to be conscious. Prejudices are being replaced by logical arguments. There is a very long way to go, but at least some salient lines of a scientific paradigm of consciousness are beginning to emerge even if these lines still need to be reconciled with one another through experimentation, logical derivation and computer simulation. This book looks not only at the qualifying necessities for conscious mechanisms but also at some of the strange things that we do with our brains that scientists and machine designers have not yet encompassed.

The designers of conscious machines.

Of course the world of conscious machines does not start and end in my own laboratory. As I write in 2005 I am aware of several major conferences on conscious machines that have brought together the thoughts and designs of others from all over the world.

So who are the conscious machine builders? For every conscious human being, being conscious is ultimately a personal affair. This makes the design of conscious machines much more of a personal quest than, say, the design of aeroplanes or computers. For example, Nobel Laureate, Gerald Edelman despite his shrewd scepticism of artificial intelligence has, with his colleagues, built a series of robots called Darwin.[5] Gerald Edelman is an expert in evolution and believes that a 'value system' is necessary for behaviour that enhances the chances of survival of the individual . A typical 'value' is 'light is better than dark to see things' or 'fear is to be avoided'. Values could be both inborn or acquired. Whatever the case, they are suitably encoded in the

[5]   Edelman, G. and Tononi, G. (2000), *A Universe of Consciousness: How Matter Becomes Imagination* (New York: Basic Books).

neural circuits of the brain to always bias the behaviour of the organism towards being in states that favour survival. Darwin III, for example, neatly learns, with a moving eye and a moving, jointed, arm that small bright objects in the field of view are important and should be touched with the tip of the arm (finger). Is Darwin conscious? Of course not, but it illustrates the usefulness of building machines to understand how concepts such as 'value' may actually contribute to the consciousness of an organism.

While not claiming to build conscious machines, the late Francis Crick with his post-Nobel interest in brains and consciousness, and Christof Koch a tireless neurobiologist at the California Institute of Technology,[6] have given machine builders a foundation on which to base their ideas. They argue, and this is one of the main premises of my own approach, that everything of which we are conscious must be reflected in the activity of some neurons in the brain. Importantly, this does not imply that we are conscious of *all* the activity of neurons in our brains. Some neurons simply act in support of others. For example (and this example will appear often in this book) Crick and Koch encourage us to believe that we are not conscious of the neural firing of our retinal cells (like photocells at the back of our eyeball) which is due to light images falling on them as in a photographic camera. If we were, we would be conscious of a jumble of scenes as might be captured by a really bad video operator who is waving his camera about. Instead, we are conscious of a coherent and solid world out there which must be the result of the firing of neurons found much deeper in the visual system, in areas where automatic compensation for eye movement takes place.

Zombies in the brain?

Indeed, the same authors refer to vast swathes of neural action of which we are *not* conscious. They call these the 'Zombie' functions of the brain.[7] Some of these zombie actions result in the

---

[6]   Crick, F and Koch, C (2003), 'A framework for consciousness', *Nature Neuroscience*, **6**, 119–126.

[7]   Koch, C. and, Crick, F. (2001), 'The zombie within', *Nature*, **411**, 893.

appropriate processing of a stimulus causing the right behaviour, without ever reaching consciousness. Cases are known of blindsight, where a person with a damaged visual system still ducks when an object is thrown at her while reporting no consciousness of the object. 'I just ducked because I felt like it' is the common explanation. A key question then arises: what physical property distinguishes zombie neurons from consciousness-generating ones? Crick and Koch used to suggest that a binding link exists between consciousness neurons. This is an oscillatory signal that is distinguished by occurring at frequency of 40 times a second. Barry Dunmall and I[8] have argued that there are alternatives to a 40 Hertz oscillation for explaining how some neurons support conscious experience and how they work together. More recently Crick and Koch have softened their belief in 40 Hertz oscillations in favour of working out how neuron groups might coalesce to create sensations. More of this in the next chapter.

Global workspaces in the brain.

Another US voice that has developed a considerable following is that of Bernie Baars, a Psychologist associated with Edelman's Neurosciences Institute in La Jolla. He speaks of a 'Global Workspace' within which some dormant memories burst into activity so as to best accommodate incoming sensory information and thus make the organism conscious of such input.[9] The selected fragments of memory control fragments of behaviour which then stimulate more input, more memories and so on. Interestingly, this somewhat abstract idea has been used by Stan Franklin of the University of Memphis to build a working system for the US Navy.[10] The system is called IDA (Intelligent Distribution Agent) and is used to communicate by email with

[8]   Aleksander, I. and Dunmall, B. (2000), 'An extension to the hypothesis of the asynchrony of visual consciousness', *Proc Royal Soc. London, B*, **267**, Number 1439 / January 22, pp. 197–200.
[9]   Baars, B. (1997), *In the Theater of Consioucness* (New York: Oxford University Press).
[10] Franklin, S. (2003), 'IDA, a conscious artefact?', *Journal of Consciousness Studies*, **10** (4–5), 47–66.

sailors to arrange the change of job that they are required to do every five years. As far as the sailors are concerned, tests on the system have shown that they react to and interact with IDA in much the same way as they would with a conscious human performing the same task. So at some level IDA passes a kind of Turing test, where its user is not sure whether it is in touch with a conscious human being or a machine.

Functional or material consciousness?

I shall argue at many points in this book, that behaviour is not a good indicator of consciousness. Nevertheless, what Stan Franklin, armed with an implementation of Bernie Baars' Global Workspace Theory, has done is to produce a machine that *functions like* living organisms we generally take to be conscious. In this sense, the machine could be said to be *functionally* conscious. This is the old story of 'if it looks like a duck, it quacks like a duck, and swims like a duck, it may as well be a duck'. My concern in this book is with another level of conscious machine, one for which I need to be convinced that there are substantial shared material properties between the machine and organisms we agree are conscious. In other words, I feel that what makes an object conscious is the important feature of it being conscious. This is being conscious in a *material* kind of way.

The builders of IDA have no misapprehensions about this. There is nowhere in IDA where one could identify a usable model of its current sensation, although there are processes that act *as if* a sensation is being used. A materially conscious machine would possess an identifiable mechanism responsible for the sensation. This, again, is something we shall discuss in the next chapter.

For the time being, it is important to note that the work on conscious machines by Edelman, Franklin and myself is by no means all that is being done in the world on conscious machines. It is sufficient however, to illustrate the difference in intentions between the functional and the material. On the whole, Edelman's and my attempts at the material level are probably less pursued than functional designs.

The emerging community

Almost on a daily basis, a new team is joining the band of designers of machines for studying consciousness. The reader may
wish to consult a recent volume of the *Journal of Consciousness
Studies* (Vol 10, no. 4–5) in which the editor, Owen Holland of the
University of Essex, ends his editorial with:

> We cannot yet know how fast and how far the enterprise will
> progress, and how much light it will be able to shed on the
> nature of consciousness itself, but it seems beyond doubt that
> machine consciousness can now take its place as a valid subject
> area within the broad sweep of consciousness studies.[11]

Poor butterfly ...

I am sure that, were he alive, clarinettist Sydney Bechet would
not mind my borrowing the title of his world-conquering tune to
say that the butterfly of thought may well be on the way to being
captured. But I am not in the business of being cruel to beautiful
butterflies. The design of materially conscious machines is a subtle business. It carries in train an increasing respect and awe of
the way that the fine mechanisms of our brains procure for us
that essential feature of our existence: the ability to think.

[11]   Holland, O. ed. (2003), *Machine Consciousness* (Exeter: Imprint Academic).

Chapter 2

The Five Tests for Being Conscious

What must a bat have to know it's a bat

There is no apparent way around the fact that the only organism I know to be truly conscious is *me*. It is true that I easily assume that others like me are also conscious, but I do not exactly know this. Magnanimously I allow that animals are conscious although I might draw a line at an amoeba. Others draw lines elsewhere. As machines get into the act things are in danger of getting even more confused.

I have already indicated in the last chapter, that conscious machines might lie between two extreme design principles: *functional* (that is, concerned with behaviour resulting from a mental state) at one end and *material* (that is, concerned with how the mental state gets there) at the other. This chapter is about materially conscious machines. That is, machines that have specialised neural mechanisms that *make* them conscious rather than mechanisms that make them *appear* to be conscious as might be the case for functionally conscious machines.

Being materially conscious

At the end of the last chapter I briefly suggested that the mechanism for arriving at material designs is through a process of introspection rather than the creation of behavioural rules. It is this idea of introspection that needs a bit of unpacking here.

Design by introspection means that I as an individual have to decide how best to break down that large number of things that go into my being conscious and decide what is most important to me. That is, which are the features of my consciousness which, if missing in the makeup of some other organism or machine, would seriously lead me to doubt whether the object was conscious. Having decided what these features are, I need to unearth whatever is known about how they arise in my nervous system to be able to understand the mechanisms and develop a design. Sometimes the neurosciences don't hold the answer and mechanisms need to be invented.

Is this 'invention' going back to writing rules for the machine? I believe not. The framework for the design of neurological mechanisms is quite different from writing rules. We shall see that it is not entirely coincidental for materially conscious machines to need this 'neurological' character. For now, suffice it to say that a neurological organism has two fundamental ways in which it differs from a computer. First, it has a highly evolved physical structure which primes it to work in ways that support thought. Second it absorbs experience rather than being given it in the form of rules. This is sometimes described as 'learning' which is a little misleading.

Not neural networks

'Learning' was the banner under which the field of 'neural networks' flourished from the early 1980s onwards. A neural network is a system of flexible cells which have an input and an output. The system is trained with examples of inputs and related outputs so that the cells can change their functions so as best to satisfy these given pairs. That is, given one of the learned inputs, the network, unaided, is expected to produce the right output. Not only this, but the net is also expected to 'generalise', that is, produce the right output for inputs that are like those that it has learned, but were not actually encountered during the training process.

For example, I show the network fifty pictures of a sheep and ask it to produce the output S and then show it another fifty pic-

tures of cows and ask it to produce the symbol C. I would then
expect a half decent neural net to produce S or C, as appropriate,
if given pictures of sheep or cows that it had seen before. But will
it give the appropriate label for new pictures of cows or sheep
that it has never seen before? If it does, then it is said to generalise. The art of designing neural networks is to get good generalisation. (The textbook I have written with Helen Morton in 1995
on neural network design addresses this art).[1]

But in talking of learning in the context of materially conscious
machines, something much more substantial that generalisation
is implied — the building up of a coherent body of experience.
Some of the architectures that build up experience, architectures
which are indeed still composed of neural cells, have been
approached in two earlier books.[2,3] Here I wish to do something
different. As mentioned earlier, getting introspection to work is
the name of the current game. We can now begin to play it.

Axioms and introspection

The rest of this chapter will deal with what for me are the five
primary pillars on which the design and functioning of a materially conscious machine can be based. I shall call these 'axioms'.
Why use a word such as 'axiom'? In mathematics this means a
clearly stated initial proposition - an assumed truth that may not
be proven, but which is sufficiently evident to support a theory.
These are the five primary elements of my sensation which I discover by looking inside myself, that is, by introspecting.

In doing this, I am entirely aware of the bad press that introspection has had in psychology. Introspection can neither be
verified nor compared among individuals. There is no way of
ascertaining that an introspective report is not just an invention.
The person who says that every time he sees the colour red he
hears a middle C played in his head, may just be lying. Given

[1]   Aleksander, I. and Morton, H.B. (1995), *An Introduction to Neural Computing*
      (London: International Thompson Computer Press).
[2]   Aleksander, I. (1996), *Impossible Minds: My Neurons My Consciousness*
      (London: Imperial College Press).
[3]   Aleksander, I. (2001), *How to Build a Mind: Machines with Imagination*
      (London: Phoenix Paperbacks).

that psychology is the study of human behaviour, the suspicion of introspection is quite correct. Any inner reports have to be confirmed and corroborated across a section of the population, before they can be incorporated into a psychological theory. In the 1950s, so called behaviourist psychologists did not even allow that some thought may be intervening between a stimulus and the organism's response to it. Any 'thought' was deemed to introduce an uncertainty into the measurement of the relationship of stimulus to response.

If, however, it is the very nature of inner sensation that is at stake, the scientific role of behaviour and thought becomes reversed. Behaviour becomes the untrustworthy parameter as the same behaviour it can be due to various thoughts. Then 'thought' has to be addressed directly. The scientist therefore is stuck with his or her own inner sensation as the starting point for an enquiry.

The introduction of the five axioms of this chapter is therefore a process of putting my inner sensation into some sort of order. For instance, the thought that goes into coping with a rapidly changing world and acting on it appropriately, is very different from, say, the thought that is evoked by a film, reading a novel or just trying to visualise where I was when Kennedy was assassinated. How different are these inner sensations? What kind of differences is one expecting to find in the neural, cellular mechanisms that support these sensations? The fact that others may agree with me that these types of thought *feel* different is sufficient to indulge in introspection and decide what major classes of sensation need to be developed into mechanisms that are properly understood.

Following a tradition started by Christof Koch and Francis Crick the neural mechanisms that are being sought are called the Neural Correlates of Consciousness (NCC). Bearing in mind what I said in the last chapter about 'consciousness' being a misleading word, an accurate description of what I am looking for are the Neural Correlates of Being Coscious or NCBC.

Correlate or identity?

What I have just expressed is not quite right. I shall be using the world 'correlate' in a much stronger way than Crick and Koch had ever intended. Indeed, what I shall be looking for is NIBC — the Neural IDENTITY of Being Conscious. Let me explain.

I shall argue that the prime objective of being conscious is being able to 'cope', in the most ample meaning of this word, with the world out there and everything that's in it. I must be able to move in the world, act on it, remember what it can do to me, control it as best I can, get what I want from it. My sensation is an inner representation among my neurons of that world out there. It must contain detail about where everything is, what things do and what they had done in the past. It must hold accurate information of what happens if I do something to this world. But the accuracy of the representation cannot be perfect. There are things I cannot see, such as ultra-violet light, things I cannot hear, such a sound frequencies above 15,000 Hertz (that is, vibrations per second). So the neural representation of the world cannot be perfect. But whatever that neural representation is, I am assuming that it is entirely responsible for my sensation of the world.

So, if I look at the empty glass to the side of my computer, every scrap of what I sense must be in this neural representation. It is almost self-evident that if there is neural representation of which I am not conscious, it falls outside the set of neural activities that I am calling the 'correlates' of my sensation. Therefore there is a total and utter correspondence between my sensation, and what some of my neurons are doing. That is, my sensation uniquely implies some neural activity and this neural activity is unique to the sensation.

To summarise, I have identified a WORLD(W) a NEURAL ACTIVITY (NA) and a SENSATION (S). The transmission from W to NA is as good as the sensory system permits. But the transmission from NA to S is perfect. Were it not, we would have to believe that sensation is somehow free from its neural activity. This, for me, is tantamount to believing in ghosts. So if I choose not to believe in ghosts, I must admit that the link between NA and S is more than a 'correlation'. In mathematics, if S is implied by NA and NA is implied by S then the relationship is called an IDENTITY. Calling it a 'correlation' is simply a way of unduly playing it safe, just in case ghosts may turn out to exist.

What now needs to be done is to look at the axioms of my sensations and begin to unravel the implications of these for the NIBC: the Neural Identity of Being Conscious. To put this less formally, looking for the NIBC is just a fancy way of asking "What goes on in my head to make me conscious".

What is neural activity?

I have somewhat glibly spoken of Neural Activity. But I am aware of the fact that not everyone is trained in neuroscience. (Those who are can easily skip this section). Keeping it as simple as possible, neurons in our heads are tiny cells (about $1/10^{th}$ of the thickness of a hair) that, when said to be active or 'to fire', produce spiky electrical impulses at the rate of about 100 per second at an output fibre that is called an axon. This fibre protrudes from a cell body which has a branch-like input end to which axons from other neurons attach. The branches are called dendrites (from 'dendros' or 'tree' in Greek) The contact between an axon and a dendritic branch is a 'synapse'.

What is called learning or adaptation occurs in the cell body and through the alterations of connection 'strengths'. It is a process whereby certain received patterns of firing from other neurons cause firing to occur reliably at the output axon. This is thought to occur as a result of alterations in the synaptic strengths in the neuron. Much of the field of 'neural networks' is devoted to modelling this neural activity and exploiting it.[1]

A list of axioms

The five axioms, the five different kinds of thought which are important to me and I feel need distinguishing are the following:

1. I feel that I am a part of, but separate from an 'out there' world.

2. I feel that my perception of the world mingles with feelings of past experience.

3. My experience of the world is selective and purposeful.

4. I am thinking ahead all the time in trying to decide what to do next.

5. I have feelings, emotions and moods that determine what I do.

This is by no means an exhaustive or, indeed, an original list. It is just an initial one, that many others have identified and may be added to in the future. But this is enough for the time being. As, in the rest of this book, we look at some of the strange things we do with our minds, the five axioms will be lurking in the background to see how they come into play in performing these mental acts.

Axiom 1 : Me in a real world out there.

What is the main thing of which I am conscious at this very moment? I am sitting in front of a computer, in a cool room. I am aware of words on its screen. I hear Dvorak's chamber music played somewhere behind me. I raise my eyes and see the printer, a heap of books a pile of papers a glass empty of water and masses of other things. I touch things, mainly the keys on the computer keyboard. I know that my bottom is reasonably cushioned from the harder part of my chair. I feel that my feet are free of my sandals and that feels comfortable. I don't smell or taste anything very much right now. I am slightly thirsty but not hungry because I have just had a salad lunch.

As I describe all this I am aware of how inadequate my description is with respect to the detail of my perception. This inner sensation is extraordinarily rich. Much richer than that which my words can covey, much richer that that which even the best equipped IMAX screen could produce. To break away from this introspective reverie, I think back to many 'pattern recognition' machines that I have built in the past and realise that whatever it is that is going on in my head is quite different from such a machine. A pattern recognition machine works as follows.

NOT pattern recognition

Pattern recognition in a machine starts with some sort of camera that turns light patterns focused by a lens onto some photosensitive surface that turns the light intensities and even colours into 'pixels'. Pixels are the little coloured dots that can be transmitted to the computer screen to make up as exact a replica of what is on the photosensitive surface. Between this photosensitive surface and the screen, the pixels exist in the computer merely as numbers. A flat image is therefore a matrix of numbers and computers are very good at doing things with matrices of numbers.

A simple but typical way for the computer to recognise patterns would be to have a few examples of classes of pictures of objects such as chairs, windows or computers stored as number matrices in its memory. Then when a new matrix appears on the photo-surface it can do a numerical comparison with the matrices stored in its memory and decide which is the most similar. The stored images are labelled so that, having found the closest one, the machine can be programmed to output, 'I am looking at a chair' or whatever is appropriate.

Now, you and I know that this is not what is happening in our heads when we report the richness of our experience. Those who hold (and I do not think there are many, but there are some) that this is how our visual consciousness works are merely illustrating how inappropriate are functional models and how the science of being visually conscious cries out for a material explanation that could plausibly encompass the true richness of what I feel and what I assume most conscious organisms feel.

I am visually conscious: tiny events

To make some headway, let me concentrate on one aspect of being conscious — the visual sensation of *me* being in the middle of an out-there world. Given that we believe in a neural activity which is identical to sensation, how could this happen? Why does the neural activity have this property of a sensation of me in an out-there world rather than some funny buzzes in my head or some sort of a headache?

I am staring at a vast white wall. Suddenly a little black fly lands on the wall, right in front of me. How do I know this? The tiny change in the world out there must have caused a tiny change in the Neural Activity, which is *identical* with my having the sensation of the littler fly on the wall.

It is possible that if the fly is tiny enough, the transmission across my visual apparatus (that is, between W and NA in terms we have encountered earlier) is just inadequate to change NA at all. I would then not 'see' the fly on the wall at all. So, it is possible to think in terms of minimal visual events which call for minimal neural activity. That is a minimal visual event is that event which, were it to be smaller or less intense, it would not be sensed at all.

Now imagine the fly shifting very rapidly slightly to the right. In slow-motion terms, the fly disappeared from where it was and reappeared somewhere nearby. I am conscious of this change. What this means is that the minimal neural activity for the new position of the fly must also be a new and unique neural activity.

Now, say, another fly, the same size as the last one lands next to the first one, but in the same position where the first one originally started. I now sense the two flies together as a separate visual event, but one which I sense as being composed of the first two. One way of achieving this is for the minimal events and the composed event just to be the firing of neurons in positions that faithfully reproduce the events in the world out there as would occur on a photosensitive surface. It would even mean that vast visual events, a waterfall, fireworks, my dog and the visitor who has just rung my doorbell could be uniquely represented in my neural system. But this would not be sufficient — what's missing is the 'out-thereness' of these neural representations of flies.

Out-thereness: depiction in the brain.

Perceiving the flies on the wall or waterfalls is different from just seeing these things as if they were photographs. Somehow or other, the neural representations, to be identical to my perceptual sensation, must be identical to this feeling of space I have around me — a space in which I can move and influence things, a space which accommodates me in the centre of it and gives me what I call my point of view.

Looking closely at what happens in the brain gives us a good clue as to how this feeling of space might arise. First, the retina at the back of the eye is not like a photographic plate in one major respect. It only records accurately (by neural firing) a very small part of the world out there. There is an area in the centre of the retina called the *fovea* that has a high density of neural sensors (cells that fire in response to the intensity of the light falling on them). If you stretch out your arm in front of you and look at your thumb, the fovea records accurately an area about the size of your thumbnail. The rest of the retina records light patterns, in much less detail, both in colour and shape. This is called the perifovea.

Now, say I am fixating on a fly with my fovea, and another fly lands nearby, the event in the perifovea, will cause my eye to move to the new event to record it accurately. By this time the first event is no longer accurately recorded in the retina, but it is in my sensation. This means that neurons in my visual system beyond the retina must not only receive signals from the fovea, but also of where the fovea is and how it has moved. Without going into details of neuroanatomy here it is well known that such areas exist in the brain. That is, my neural activity for visual consciousness relies as much on what the fovea records as where the fovea is and how it moves.

Not only this, but when objects are closer or farther, this too is recorded as a result of the muscular mechanisms for eye convergence and focus. That is neurons responsible for giving me my sensation receive signals from muscles involved in eye positioning and shape. It is even known that neurons that drive muscles used in touching a seen object or are just preparing to move a finger to touch it broadcast firing signals that influence the firing of neurons that create sensation. No wonder that my visual sensation of the world out there is much richer than a photograph - its neural identity is extraordinarily rich. Barry Dunmall and I have called this inner identity of neural activity a *depiction*. Fig 2.1 should help to illustrate how depiction works.

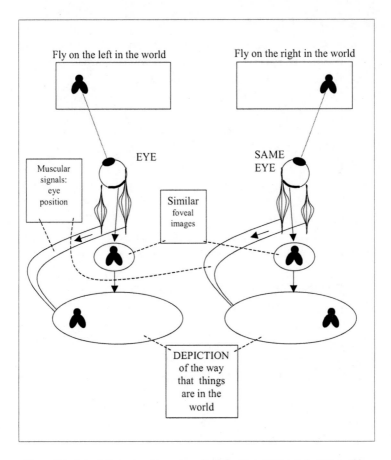

Figure 2.1: A depiction arises in an area where the foveal image is 'positioned' by the muscular signals that indicate eye position.

We chose *depiction* to get away from the word *representation* because of the richness that the neural activity implies. A photograph is a representation and, in computing, just symbols could be used to represent objects in the world (F for fly or F2 for another fly). Representations therefore have a functional character about them while I intend *depiction* to mean the full rich material quality that is required for being conscious.

Evidence: locking

Is all this reliance on depiction just a theory or is there evidence that it actually happens in living conscious organisms? In fact, the evidence is overwhelming and continually being discovered. As I have suggested, depiction occurs because some cells are selected to fire only if muscles are being active in a particular way. In neurology, this selection process is called 'locking'.

Locking was first discovered as 'gaze locking' in an area of the brain called V3A which represents the form of visual stimuli This was the pioneering work of Galletti and Battaglini from the University of Bologna.[4] They found that certain cells in monkeys would respond to small visual stimuli, but only if the eyes of the monkey were pointing in a particular direction. If the monkey would change its direction of gaze, different cells would respond to the same stimulus.

The same laboratory went on to discover even more evidence of locking. For example, neurons in visual area V6 (devoted to space representation) will only fire if certain arm muscles are engaged in moving the arm in a particular way . Other neurons in another part of the visual system are locked to neck muscle action. The fashion for looking for locked neurons has spread to other laboratories and these have been found in profusion throughout the cerebral cortex (i.e. the part that is deeply implicated in making us conscious).

Other senses

Above, I have chosen the most depictive of senses, vision, to illustrate depiction. What happens in the case of the other senses? The next most depictive sense is touch. Through touch we also develop depictive spaces in our brains that are similar to those of vision. That is, we can create neural maps of what is around us, again from a central point of view. Of course, it is also apparent that the visual and tactile maps integrate to depict the world out there. A simple experiment is to touch the rim of a glass or a cup with the index finger and the one next to it. All

[4]   Galletti, C. and Battaglini, P. (1989), 'Gaze-dependent visual neurons in area V3A of monkey', *J. Neurosci*, **9**, 1112–1125.

seems normal – the cup feels just how it looks. Then cross these two fingers and do it again. The rim feels strangely double. The positioning of the tactile signal in a depictive neural surface in the brain has been fooled!

Hearing is the next most depictive sense, but it is not as accurate as the first two. Stereo audition works because there are some neurons in the auditory system of the brain which only respond to specific 'phase' differences of the pressure waves that reach one's ears. If a sound source is off-centre there are tiny delays in the way that the sound reaches one ear with respect to the other. This is a phase difference. The 'out-thereness' of audition comes from the fact that head movements affect this phase difference offering the opportunity for muscular locking similar to the case of eye movement. Of course, evolution has made sure that this too integrates with the earlier two senses, to provide the richest possible depiction of the 'out-there' world.

Smell and taste in humans are hardly depictive at all. Of course I am not arguing that we are not conscious of these, it is just that their mechanisms are less involved in the sensation that is the subject of Axiom 1, the sensation of an out there world. We can just about work out where a smell of a burning cigarette is coming from, while taste always comes from the same areas of the tongue. We are not conscious of the position of taste on the tongue despite the fact that different tastes come from different areas.

The centrality of axiom 1.

The ability to internalise the out-there world is, in my opinion, the central feature of consciousness: it is a kind of pivot on which all else depends. I bear this in mind when considering the other axioms and their implied mechanisms, perhaps not lingering on them quite as much as on axiom 1.

Axiom 2: my experience of the world out there

Staying again with visual sensation for a while, it is clear that, if I close my eyes, the visual world does not go away: I can imagine what things look like, that is, what they looked like at some time in the past. The sensation is not quite as vivid as when I am actually looking at something, but there nonetheless.

These 'visions' need not go away when I do open my eyes. Indeed they are part of my visual interaction with the world out there. I often loose my keys. When looking for them under cushions or behind the toaster I form a mental image of what they will look like when I do see them. If I should see a different bunch of keys, the differences between the depiction of these and the mental image are intensely, almost painfully, felt. When seeing a well known face, it is known that I can form a sufficiently appropriate mental image of the person even before my fovea has had a chance to look at every feature. That is, the mental image snaps in.

There is another aspect to these inner sensations: they can construct something we may never have seen or experienced. Reading Shakespeare's Macbeth, the full impact of Birnam Wood descending on Dunsinane is generated in our visual sensation even if we have never seen the play. This is a case where visions are generated by words, but visions could be generated by any of the sensory modalities: the smell of freshly baked bread can trigger scenes from childhood, touching a slimy surface in the dark can create nightmarish visions of unpleasant gutters.

The neural identity of experience

The material implication of these inner visions and memories is, in broad terms, quite simple. In detail it is fascinating and difficult. The broad principle is that of *feedback* or *re-entry* in depictive neural structures. Having a mental image of something that has happened in the past has a strong material implication: closed information paths in depictive networks must exist which can *sustain* depictive firing patterns. Take this simple example. Three neurons, A, B, C with one synapse (input) and one axon (output) each are connected to one another like a string of three beads, A to B and B to C. Say that they have all learned to fire when their synapse receives firing and not to fire when the synapse is not receiving firing. If A's input is now stimulated, all three neurons will fire, while if A's input is not stimulated no neuron will fire.

Now we connect the output of C back to A (this is feedback or re-entrance) notice that if anything stimulates any of the inputs for any length of time, all three will fire and continue firing until something turns one of them off and then they will all turn off. This simple system has two mental images: all on or all off. A depictive area of the brain can learn to sustain images provided that there are sufficient interconnections between neural inputs and outputs. Under 'thinking ahead' below, we shall come back to these three neurons and look at how they can recall changing images.

So much for the mechanism of sustaining images, but where does what we imagine come from? How could it be that having seen examples of black dogs and white cats, we could imagine what a white dog or a black cat might look like even though we may never have seen one. The fact that we can do this implies that blackness and whiteness might be depicted and learned in different parts of the mechanism from, say, shape. Indeed, it is well known that, in the brain, different areas of the visual cortex become independently active for colour, shape and motion.

Then whiteness or any other colour-ness, is learned to be a stable depiction and associated with words in one part of the cortex while doggy-ness or catty-ness is learned in another. Then these learned features will be depicted independently if triggered by appropriate words even if the combination has never been seen before.

Two questions arise here. How are depictions tied to words and language? This is a huge question which, in this book can only be briefly addressed (Chapter 8). The second puzzle is, if depictions such as colour and shape happen in different parts of the brain, how is it that a black cat, say, *feels* like a single sensation? This, in neurology, is called *the binding problem*.

Unwinding the binding problem

All sorts of solutions have been proposed to the binding problem. Crick and Koch, for example, first maintained that a signal with a firing rate of 40 pulses per second links any disparate activities that bind into one sensation.[5] They now prefer to talk of cell assemblies that 'coalesce' into single sensations through long-routed connections.[6]

My colleague Barry Dunmall and I have suggested[7] that binding is a direct result of the muscular *locking* that I mentioned earlier in this chapter. Going back to the fly on the white wall imagine that the fly could be red or blue. What happens when the fly is red? To simplify the rather complex way that colour and shape are represented in the visual cortex, I shall just call these two areas C and S. Whether the fly is red or blue, it will cause a group of cells to fire in S, and these cells are *locked* by the position of the fly on the wall. The fly, if only S were present, would feel like a blob in a particular out-there position. In C, however, two different groups of neurons would be activated one for the blue fly and the other for a red one. But whether blue or red they would all be locked by the position of the fly on the wall. The fact that this *feels* like a coloured blob in exactly the same place on the wall as the activity in S is due to the fact that, due to locking, the two activities are controlled by where in the world is the event that is causing them. This is the beauty and the cause of richness of the depictive process — the neurons causing a single sensation could be dispersed among different specialised parts of the brain.

Binding in imagination

Of course, the binding problem applies to the basic depictive process of axiom 1. How does it affect axiom 2: imagination? The depictive areas in which I have suggested feedback creates the ability to reconstruct visual images (say) occur physically beyond the locking process. That is, what is remembered are 'out

[5]   Crick, F. and Koch, C. (1998), 'Consciousness and neuroscience', *Cereb Cortex*, **8** (2), 97–107.
[6]   Crick, F. and Koch, C. (2003), 'A framework for consciousness', *Nature Neuroscience*, **6**, 119–126.
[7]   Aleksander, I. and Dunmall, B. (2000), 'An extension to the hypothesis of the asynchrony of visual consciousness', *Proc Royal Soc. London, B*, **267** (1439), 197–200.

there' depictions. The only odd thing is that during a proper recall of an out-there events, many depictive areas are required to deliver their memories at once.

This process is not perfect. It is quite possible to be in a situation where we remember the shape of, say, a hat that the Queen was wearing in a newsreel of Ascot last week but cannot remember its colour, or vice versa — remember the colour and not the shape.

Other senses and experience

Interestingly the vividness of our memory in other senses seems to rank in the same way as their depictiveness. The link between touch and building up memories of what has been touched (particularly important in those who have poor or missing sight) proves to be as powerful as vision.

Audition comes next. We can generally 'hear tunes in our heads', which must be due to depictive patterns, stimulated in much the same way as visual ones: by words or other sensory input. If someone says 'Beethoven's Fifth' to me, I can immediately hear the pattern of the four opening timpani beats that are so well associated with this symphony: Ta Ta Ta Tammmm ... Ti Ti Ti Tommmm. Talking of Beethoven, deaf as he was, he could still hear his compositions in his head and write them down. Orchestra conductors would be lost without having depictions of the sounds they expect to hear present in their heads from memory or stimulated by the score in front of them.

Smell and taste are the hardest to remember, and they are the lowest on the depiction list. While we can remember how to label smells and tastes once we experience them, we cannot easily 'feel them in our heads'. Indeed, axiom 2 implies rather strongly: 'no depiction and no feedback — then no imagination'.

Axiom 3: Out to get experience

So far, I have spoken of worlds out there as if the conscious organism just blunders around in them. Nothing is further from the truth. Selecting what we experience in the world and how we think about the world in our imagination, requires some selection mechanisms. This, in neurology and psychology, is called 'attention'.

In recent years attention has advanced in importance as a vital aspect of consciousness. Our tendency to attend to some things and not others determines what eventually enters our consciousness — a topic scrutinised closely in Chapter 6. There we shall see that, in vision in particular, specific brain areas such as the 'superior colliculus' are involved in the attentive selection of eye position for the most efficient extraction of meaning from complex images. Suffice it to say here that we have already noted that movement of the fovea contributes to depiction. Attention appears to call for important axiomatic mechanisms: it has been hailed by several investigators as the 'Gateway to Consciousness'.

Axiom 4: Thinking ahead

Thought is not just a process of having static depictions. It is a highly dynamic process. We are constantly thinking ahead, considering alternatives and, every now and then, deciding what to do next. What are the material implications of this possibility.

In fact, no new machinery needs to be evoked over and above that which we have seen in axiom 2: re-entrant neural networks. Going back to the string of neurons A, B and C with C re-entering to A, we can show that even this simple system can remember sequences as well as the stationary patterns we have seen above. As before, the neurons repeat at the output axon the state of the input synapse. It helps to realise that there is always a slight delay between a change in input (say of duration t) and the corresponding change of output.

Now let us imagine that A has just come on with the other two off (ABC = 100, in binary talk). After some time t this changes to 010, then to 001 and 100 and so on. A similar sequence of patterns could be 110, 011, 101, 110 … In the old days[8] this used to be called a reverberatory circuit. Much of the brain's inner activity was thought to be due to the setting up of appropriate reverbera-

---

[8]   Hebb, D.O. (1949), *The Organisation of Behaviour* (New York: Chapman and Hall).

tory neural circuits. All I have done is to use the idea to demonstrate that a neural circuit can remember sequences of depictions
as well as static ones. But the process of thinking ahead is much
more than the reverberation of a neural net.

I am looking at a pencil on my desk and deciding that I want to
pick it up. This thought is a sensation of my actually doing it in
my head, before I do it for real. My depictive areas are producing
a kind of depicted movie in my head in anticipation of the real
act. This comes from the fact that the depictive areas can learn
appropriate depictive sequences as part of the build-up of experience as a sequence of depictive states. That is, as a child I learn
to pick things up by trial and error. When I succeed reliably, my
visual, tactile and muscular neurons have, together, learned to
go from state to state by the same axiom 2 mechanism that allows
them to remain stable in one state. There is very little technical
difference between learning sequences and learning single
stable states.

In our little example of three neurons a state transition might
be 100 to 010. But a vast re-entrant neural network could have
depictive state transitions from a hand at rest to the states that
are met on the way to picking up an object. So thinking ahead has
to do with the system running through depictive sequences that
are possible from the current state. But if there are many possi-
bilities how are these controlled? What is it to *want* to execute
one of the possible plans? This leads to axiom 5.

Axiom 5: Emotions – *the guardians of thought*

One of the criticisms levelled at those who speak of conscious
machines is that there is one element of humanity that machines
cannot have: feelings and emotions. I would argue that as these
seem to be essential to being a conscious human being they must
be essential to being a conscious machine. I would be very suspi-
cious of the consciousness of a machine were it not to have mechanisms that play the role of emotions in living organisms.

In the first instance emotions are related to the evaluation of
depictive input. Children not more than a few hours old will
show signs of fear (facial expression and a retreating action) if a

large object moves towards them. The same occurs if the child is allowed to move freely over a glass surface that appears to stretch over a precipice. The child avoids the precipice and shows signs of fear. On the other hand the child shows content-ment on being fed when hungry. So, basic emotions such as fear and pleasure, are neural activities that appear to be pre-wired at birth. They have obvious survival value. Other emotions in this innate group are anger, surprise, disgust and love.

Other emotions and feelings are developed during perceptual life. Feeling hurt after being rebuked or being jealous of the attention someone else is getting are examples of a vast group of such subtle phenomena. On the basis that every scrap of our sen-sation is due to some neural firing patterns, I would expect such patterns to have distinct characteristics that both adapt to be attached to perceptual depictive events as well as imagined events. As planning proceeds according to the mechanisms of axiom 4, predicted states of the world trigger emotional neural firing which determines which plans are preferred for execution and which might lead to unwanted consequences.

Volition and emotion is another area that has proved to be controversial. Not only does the question of free will have a theological and philosophical theory, but in modern neurology some doubts have arisen as to whether we are in wilful control of all our actions. This is the material of Chapter 7. But one thing is sure, an organism without neural mechanisms for conscious emotional evaluation of thoughts and plans would have its capacity for survival strongly curtailed. I have always had my suspicions about Mr Spock in the old Star Wars. The idea of logic without emotion would not have stopped his ancestors from falling off precipices before the logic had a chance to cut in.

The moral of the axiomatic story

The main reason for presenting the axioms as sequences going from a felt inner sensation to a generating mechanism that may both be found in the brain and act as a design principle for a con-scious machine, is to stress an important point. It argues that there need not be any insurmountable gaps in this sequence. If sensation implies mechanism then it at least seems feasible to assume mechanism implies sensation. The two are as inseparable as the presence of H_2O molecules implying that water is present and the presence of water implying the H_2O molecules are present. To seek a science that says that the two are separated by an explanatory gap is bizarre. For me to seek a science that separates sensation from the action of its material mechanism seems equally bizarre.

Chapter 3

Sleep, Dreams and the Unconscious

What happens when we are not conscious?

I, in common with the entire mammalian species, am happy to surrender the gift of consciousness at least once a day for a satisfying period of sleep. Sometimes during sleep I dream. On the whole the dreams I remember are unremarkable but feel real. So when they take on a bizarre form, they must be doing something different from what waking perception and memory do. Where waking experience enables me to understand and make use of the world out there in as accurate a way as possible, the dream presents me with fictional realities. I say fictional, but often they contain elements of reality put together in strange ways.

The night before a public lecture I dreamt that I was giving the lecture. In the dream I was even able to see my slides clearly. But suddenly I realised that I was wearing nothing below my waist. The planning in my dream was quite accurate: I would stay behind the podium as long as possible and then flee pulling my shirt as far down as it would go. What possible role could this type of consciousness play in the leading of my waking life? What mechanisms of cellular activity could be causing this? Are dreams necessary for the proper functioning of conscious mechanisms or are they just a whimsical by-product of the functioning of these mechanisms? These are the questions addressed in this chapter. The interested reader should consult one of the many texts that may be found on this subject that present the technical details of sleep and dreaming.[1,2] Here I shall summarise some of this, but ask a slightly different question: what might be happening to our axiomatic depictive mechanisms of consciousness during sleep?

It is the bizarre nature of dreams that has given them a special place in almost every culture of the world. They have been treated as predictions of the future, as omens, as links with the dead and links to divinity. They are sometimes seen as windows on better and more desirable worlds. We speak of a dream car or a dream holiday. So what could contribute more directly to dualist notions about consciousness than these ethereal constructions that appear to come from nowhere to create our nightly consciousness? Where do the axioms of the mechanisms of being conscious stand when it comes to sleeping and dreams?

If dreams are strange, so are parts of the night when I sleep without dreaming. How does this lack of consciousness differ from being in a coma, being anaesthetised or, even being dead? Death or 'the long sleep' must surely be distinguished from dreamless sleep where, despite not being conscious of anything, my brain has not stopped working. Surely if we can discover the mysterious switch in the brain that makes it go from dreamless sleep to conscious dreams then here we have a mechanism that reveals a great deal about how we become conscious. Then another focusing question for this chapter is whether a conscious machine would *need* to sleep and dream, and how this can throw light on the necessity of the strange phenomenon of dreaming.

Sigmund Freud notably defined the existence of an 'unconscious' — a kind of repository of thoughts that have curiously been cut off from being accessed during normal wakeful thinking.[3] This gave dreams a highly useful function: 'dreams are the royal road to a knowledge of the unconscious mind'. So dreams became an investigative tool in the psychoanalyst's armoury.

[1]   Cartwright, R.D. (1978), *A Primer on Sleep and Dreaming* (London: Addison Wesley).
[2]   Bootzin, R.R., Khilstrom, J.F. and Schachter, D.L., ed. (1990), *Sleep and Cognition* (Washington: APA).
[3]   Freud, S. (1955) *The Interpretation of Dreams* (New York: Basic Books).

Later in this chapter we shall see that 'the unconscious' makes sense as a technological concept and that designers of conscious machines may need to be aware of the possibility that a machine could develop an unconscious mind.

Why sleep?

Memories of late nights swatting for exams or flagging after a long dinner party provide one kind of an answer: we sleep to relieve tiredness and tiredness is that internal sensation that tells us that our bodies are in need of temporary relief from having expanded too much energy. Lack of sleep would cause us to burn out too fast. Small creatures that sleep a lot live for a long time. A bat, I am told, sleeps 20 hours a day and lives 18 years while a shrew of roughly the same weight as a bat sleeps very little and only lives for 2 years. So the simple explanation of sleep is to conserve energy and to prolong life.

This is not a foreign thought to machine designers. My conscious robot on Mars may need to have periods of sleep during which it can recharge its batteries through the use of its solar cells. So, like the bat, its periods of sleep may have to happen during the day. But in living biological organisms the recharging of batteries is effectively done by intake such as breathing and food. Sleep is necessary for the purpose of taking off physical load from action organs (muscles, primarily) so that energy can be absorbed from the fuel and that self repair of stressed material can take place. Non-living machines may not need this on a daily basis, although the regular service of cars, aeroplanes and lawn-mowers is known to prolong active life and avoid breakdowns. Of course, self-repair does not happen and mechanics need to be called in. The beauty of living organisms is that they largely do not need external agencies to effect the service: they do it by a process of relaxation. If a muscle is under tension during the day, it needs the lack of demand at night to return to a repaired state in which, the next day it can begin work again. Sleep therefore seems to be a regular event that allows this to happen.

The brain and sleep

More than wakeful consciousness, where at least it is possible to ask people what is on their minds, the unconscious brain or the dreaming brain appear to be secret and disturbingly intangible. This makes an experimental science of sleep and dreaming difficult. Or, at least, it did until in 1892 when George Trumball Ladd of Yale University noticed that a sleeping child, during specific periods of its slumber, would begin to move its eyes under closed lids.[4] Almost as an inspired guess, Ladd suggested that this was due to the child 'looking at its dreams'.

Not much else was done until it was shown in the 1920s that an instrument called the electroencephalograph (EEG) could measure internal electrical activity of the brain. This instrument measures very slight voltage differences between electrodes placed in selected positions on the scalp. In the 1930s these machines began to be used to measure brain rhythms during sleep. Generally, electrodes are placed so as to measure autonomous wavelike brain activity, eye movement and muscular tonus (or tension). It is the change in patterns of these three electrical measurements that indicated that sleep proceeded in a series of distinct phases.

It was in 1953 that Nathaniel Kleitman and his graduate student Eugene Aserinsky at the University of Chicago noted that rapid eye movements (REM) during sleep were seen to be an important recurring characteristic of the various patterns of combined brain activity that develop during a night's sleep[5]. Returning to the idea that this might have something to do with dreaming they began to wake up their participants during REM sleep and when REM was absent. Their suspicions were right: those waking out of REM sleep were much more likely to report that they had been dreaming and what the dream was about than those whose eyes had not been moving (non-REM sleep or NREM). The remarkable feature of REM encephalographic recordings is their similarity to those of awake participants.

---

[4]   Ladd, G. (1982), 'Contributions to the psychology of visual dreams', *Mind*,**1**, 299–304.

[5]   Aserinsky, E and Kleitman, N. (1953), 'Regular periods of eye motility and concomitant phenomena during sleep', *Science*, **118**, 273.

The important implication of this is that the experimenter can note the point at which the brain switches from a much attenuated consciousness to the dream. Woken from NREM, participants might report rather bland and vague thoughts such as 'I may have been vaguely thinking of a pear'. In contrast, while in REM the reports are more imaginative and story-like, possibly with a bizarre twist: 'I was waiting for my deceased grandmother in the Zoo, then a large rat, the size of a horse spoke to me to say that my granny could not make it.' The dualist notion of a dream unrelated to neural firing begins to lose ground as here is a clear material indication of a profound change of an inner conscious state that engenders a dream. Some may say that the glamour of a dream is being destroyed by this type of science. I disagree, it merely heightens the need to understand how and why the brain presents us with an imagined reality during the night without removing the wonder that we might have for this phenomenon.

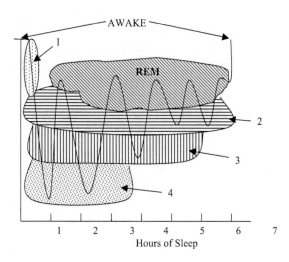

Figure 3.1: The stages of sleep

Nightly rhythms

The patterns of EEG from the different measurements mentioned above (eye movement, brain wave and muscle tonus) have been classified into different stages that are distinguished as follows. Figure 3.1 might help to visualise what appears to be happening during a typical night. The wavy line indicates a path taken in time through different stages by the brain

> *Awake:* the eyes move in an irregular way and are susceptible to perceptual or even auditory input. The brain generates waves that are characteristic of wakefulness, the so called 'alpha' rhythms — about 10 cycles per second. The facial muscles are alert with a measurable tonus.
>
> *Stage 1:* Just as the person falls asleep, the eye movements become slow and regular with a side-to-side motion while brain waves show less alpha rhythm, muscle tonus being much the same as in the awake stage. This stage lasts only a few minutes.
>
> *Stage 2:* The main change is noticed in the brain wave which becomes more rapid than the alpha rhythm and is called a 'spindle' by sleep neurologists. The sleeper is susceptible to external input which shows up in both the brain wave and eye movement as a 'jolt' that disturbs the more rhythmic activity. Muscles are less tensioned than in stage 1. This lasts for a little longer than stage 1 sleep and changes gradually to stage 3.
>
> *Stage 3:* This is characterised by the appearance of powerful but slow brain waves, muscles relaxing further and eyes moving with slow random movement. The muscles continue to relax. After 10 or so minutes, this leads to stage 4.
>
> *Stage 4:* This is the first settled period of sleep that can last for 45 or so minutes. Slow brain waves are well established, muscles relatively relaxed and eye movements are slow and oblivious to external or internal stimulation.

Then a strange thing happens, and the sleeper starts climbing backward through stages 3 and 2 but instead of going through 1 to become awake, REM sleep is briefly encountered.

This is recognised by the characteristic rapid eye movement. While the muscles in the head and neck are relaxed, other physiological factors become very active: heart rate rises, breathing becomes more rapid and genital enlargement can take place in males. But the sleeper only samples this state for a few minutes before plunging down to the more restful stage 4. As shown, the see-saw action returns to REM sleep typically another four times, spending longer in this condition each time. The last visit leads to awakening and if dreams occur during this last REM period they are the most likely ones to be remembered.

It is known that adults spend about a quarter of their sleeping time in REM sleep, whereas babies do so for longer periods of up to 50% of their sleep. Psychologists read some suggested REM functions into this, as we shall see next.

What is REM sleep for ?

While it is difficult to have a *proven* theory as to why REM sleep and dreaming have evolved, there are many hypotheses about the excursions into REM sleep as in fig 3.1. Some have suggested that this prepares the 'higher brain centres' to process ever increasing amounts of sensory information that has to be absorbed into experience[6] while others postulate that this places the organism into a state of readiness from time to time, should action need to be taken. This is in contrast with slumbering in stage 4 for too long from which it is hard to awake and spring into full activity.[7] Many have suggested informational models (the need for time to transfer data from short to long term memory, or consolidate learned information). Towards the end of this chapter I shall suggest a more elaborate informational model based on the depictive axioms of being conscious.

It is very difficult to confirm or deny any hypotheses about the role of REM sleep and associated dreaming. In an effort to provide evidence for such hypotheses attempts have been made since 1960 to deprive willing participants of REM sleep,[8] only to discover that the brain would fight such attempts and cast those tested into ever more frequent REM periods. In other words it is difficult to cut REM sleep out of the sleep cycle without seriously depriving participants of sleep altogether. Some REM depriva-

---

[6]   Roffwarg,, H., Muzio, J. and Dement, W. (1966), 'Ontogenic development of the human sleep-dream cycle', *Science*, **152**, 604–619.

[7]   Snyder, F. (1966), 'Towards an evolutionary theory of dreaming', *American Journal of Psychiatry,* **123**, 121–136.

[8]   Dement, W. (1960), 'The effect of dream deprivation', *Science*, **131**, 1705–1707.

tion experiments showed that there might be an increased tendency to fantasize both during sleep and during waking hours.[9]

So whatever the explanation, REM and dreaming appear to be essential to the make up of the human being and possibly to all members of the mammal kingdom. There is no shortage of existing theories of the purpose of dreams for us to look at.

Freud's access to the unconscious

Probably the most celebrated among theories of the purpose of dreams is that of Freud[3]. Freud's beliefs about dreams centre on the existence of an 'unconscious'. This is a repository of thoughts and memories which, despite being engendered during wakeful consciousness, become inaccessible during later waking periods. This, he believed, is where 'repressed' thoughts go, that is thoughts that are so unacceptable to the waking mind, that they need to be locked away so as not to distort an untroubled waking life. During sleep, he notes, the sleeper is largely immobilised and therefore safe from being able to act on inappropriate thoughts or repressed desires. So it is safe for such thoughts to emerge in the guise of dreams.

But these dreams are not direct representations of the repressed thoughts. They are disguised and it is their interpretation that relieves the dreamer of the burden of carrying unreachable mental baggage. For this reason some psychoanalysts discuss their clients' dreams with them and attempt to interpret them. For example, a female patient may be disturbed by the appearance of a cypress tree in her dream which seems to be unduly menacing and attractive at the same time. The psychoanalyst may explore with her the cliché possibility of this being a phallic desire for a forbidden liaison. I shall return later in this chapter to the notion that a machine might have an unconscious mind and how this might arise.

[9]   Cartwright, R. and Ratzel, R. (1972), 'Effects of dream loss on waking behaviors', *Archives of General Psychiatry*, **27**, 277–280.

Spring-cleaning theories

Many sleep researchers have suggested that dreams have a role of somehow 'tidying-up' the memory circuits of the brain. Some believe that dreams help to straighten out waking thoughts while others simply suggest that some unconscious sorting of memories goes on. For example, an influential corpus of work due to Louis Breger[10] then of the California Institute of Technology, suggests that the frequent occurrence of dreams that represent recent experience means that this is the brain's way of incorporating new experience into its collection of previous memories and making sure that contradictions are smoothed out. This, he believes, is particularly noticeable with experiences with a strong emotional content. Meeting a potential new lover may lead to vivid dreams of intercourse with this person to allow the memory structures of the brain to adjust to this idea even if it has not happened in reality.

Others who have followed this style of analysis have suggested that this is also a way for the brain to deal with stressful thoughts. They suggest that the brain becomes better able to cope with difficulties after a night of assimilation and significant REM sleep. Rosalind Cartwright has done studies with divorced women and has shown that those participants who exhibited normal sleep patters of long an positive dreams were coping better and were less depressed than others whose sleep patterns were disturbed.[11] She concludes that 'Dreaming is involved in reviewing, organising and rehearsing conceptions of who we are and how we are doing in our own eyes'.

Accidental dreams?

Neurophysiologists have suggested that activity in a brain area called the pontine-geniculate-occipital (PGO) may be associated with a variety of dream characteristics including their vividness and bizarreness. This could suggest that REM, rather than being

[10]   Breger, L. (1969), 'Dream function: an information processing model'. In L. Breger (Ed.), *Clinical-Cognitive Psychology* (New Jersey: Prentice-Hall).
[11]   Cartwright, R.D. (1990), 'A network model of dreams'. In Bootzin et al. (ed.), *Sleep and Cognition*, chapter 13.

an indication of coherent night time thought, is the consequence of a physiological event which at the same time stimulates 'thought' areas of the brain. This creates a debate on whether it is the cognitive behaviour of the brain that determines dream content or whether dream content is merely an accidental outcome of a physiological event in the brain.

A model that takes this PGO activity into account is that of Hobson and McCarley first advocated in 1977 and later elaborated in many ways.[12] This suggests that random activity from the PGO stimulates the cortex at random, and the cortex then associates these random inputs with the nearest experiences current at the time of going to sleep. Therefore the results of the random action are not random in themselves but reflect some aspects of waking reality.

Another influential theoretical strand is due to Crick and Mitchison.[13,14] Their model suggested that rather than assimilating new memories, dreaming is a purging exercise which rids the brain of unwanted memories to make room for new ones. Dreams in this process are incidental and seen as useless material that needs to be purged. The model involves the effect of noise in a neural network, an idea that I shall explore next in this chapter but not as a spring-cleaning activity, but rather as a resetting action to prepare the brain for new work.

Do depictive automata need to dream?

Here I shall develop the idea that sleep is a necessary feature and dreaming a possible outcome of this in a class of machines driven by depictive automata as defined in chapter 2. While this class includes the biological, for illustration I have in mind a robot that has been sent to a distant planet to explore and send important data back to earth. During the waking, working day,

[12] Hobson, J.A. and McCarley, R.W. (1977), 'The brain as a dream generator: An activation-synthesis hypothesis of the dream process', *American Journal of Psychiatry*, **134**, 1335–1348.

[13] Crick, F. and Mitchison, G. (1983), 'The function of dream and sleep', *Nature*, **304**, 111–114.

[14] Crick, F. and Mitchison, G. (1986), 'REM sleep and neural nets', *Journal of Mind and Behaviour*, **7**, 229–250.

it has targets either recalled from its imaginative cellular apparatus (axiom 2) or perceived from a transmission from earth. It uses its planning ability (axiom 4) to assess these tasks or, to use a metaphor, to assess how it feels about various things that could be done (axiom 5). This is done within an imaginative awareness of the 'world out there' as ascertained by axiom 2.

The power resources of this robot (say batteries) are limited and need recharging for a good period while no demands are being made of them. That is, the robot must shut down as much of its activity as possible for this recharging to take place so that the mission can be stretched as far as possible over time. Of course robots could be designed in different ways — charging could take place during work cycles, but this robot is designed not only to provide information on the structure of the planet it is exploring but also to address the question 'what might it be like to be an astronaut on this planet' in the style of 'what is it like to be a bat?'. As hinted in several places in this book, the important subsidiary question is 'what does a robot (astronaut) need to have to know what it can and will do?'.

The mind cannot be shut down

Like a living being, this robot does not have permanent storage facilities that can hold information (in contrast to my laptop, say, that has magnetic discs and a writeable CD ROM). Is this the result of technological ignorance on my part? Perhaps not. The mind of this robot is based on a depictive-axiomatic design which means that its memory is ensured by a structure as shown in Fig. A7 of appendix A2. Therefore memory of both daily events and past experience is stored as individual functions of the cells in re-entrant networks. This means that waking thought is equivalent to *being* in some sequence of conscious states.

To keep the energy expenditure at a minimum, the system cannot lose whatever source of energy keeps the function of cells in place, (that would mean brain death) while its ability to pursue state trajectories needs to be curtailed as part of the falling asleep process. A direct way would be simply to hold the system in the last 'thought' state it had found during waking.

Being in 'neutral' when waking up

Holding the last waking state may not be the best thing for the organism. The new working period may bring new learning and working challenges — it may not be good to be stuck at the end of the last working state trajectory. So it is desirable for the machine to have a kind of 'neutral' waking up state from which either previous thoughts can be resumed, new thoughts freely entered or even new experiences laid down.

Readers who frequently use computers may be tempted to draw an analogy here: a computer can be shut down either in a 'standby' state where, on switching on, the work that was being done on shut down can immediately be resumed. Alternatively, the computer can be 'shut down' completely, so that when switched on it is ready to do something new. To my mind, this is a slightly misleading metaphor. The depictive/axiomatic machinery is not a massive filing cabinet like a computer, that simply makes sure that all jobs are stored in files that are then picked out if and when necessary. A file can be kept in the working space or put away. What makes our robot conscious is the vast number of trajectories that the machinery can perform. They are not stored anywhere, they are created as and when required by the adapted functions of its large number of cells. So in order to get into 'neutral' the depictive machinery might have to 'skip' through some possible thought trajectories. Is this skipping what dreaming and REM sleep are all about? What could be the nature of the mechanisms that cause this 'skipping' to happen?

In summary, we have identified two requirements for sleep in the thought (axiom 2) module of a depictive/axiomatic brain: first being in a largely inactive state akin to NREM sleep in living organisms for some of the time. Second, making sure that on waking, the mechanism is in good shape for the waking hours to come. How can both these requirements be met?

Anaesthesia may provide a hint

The problem is to imagine how a very active piece of machinery which is darting about its imaginational plans can be stopped and then lulled into a beneficial neutral state. First, the thinking part of the brain (the cortex in living organisms, axiom 2 machinery in the robot) needs to be protected from sensory input and prevented from activating the musculature. This would leave such machinery in a state from which it was free to skip over trajectories to find the necessary neutral state. But this still implies an undue expenditure of energy. The hint of how the robot could reduce its thinking activity to a minimum presented itself in discussion with Geoff Lockwood an anaesthetist colleague at the Hammersmith Hospital in London.

Apparently, brain modules can be prevented from pursuing their state trajectories by anaesthetics that reduce the generalising properties of the cells. The key functions of a cell whether in the brain or in a depictive machine (Appendix A1) is first to learn how to react to a set of input patterns and then to respond in appropriate ways to patterns similar to the learned ones. The latter property is called generalisation. In modules, where cells are sensitive to the output of other cells, it is this property that creates 'attractors' (appendix A2). That is, the module may have learned to remain stable in some cycle of states representing a thought, and this cycle is triggered by one element of the thought. For example, the thought of going to work in my car in the morning could trigger the thought of where I parked the car last night.

Generalisation allows a whole series of similar thoughts to trigger the right trajectory and also causes the trajectory to recover should it be disturbed by the aberrations of some of the cells or by what in telephones, amplifiers and televisions is called 'electrical noise'. So, if the generalisation of the cells in a module is reduced, the attractors disappear without the function of the cells being lost, only to restore the attractors when generalisation returns.

Anaesthetists go to a lot of trouble to point out that being under an anaesthetic is not at all like being asleep. There are no REM episodes and only very rarely are dreams reported. What does happen at times is that sensory data, mainly auditory, breaks through into awareness and is stored like a waking memory. Anaesthetists dread this, as a patient who remembers the

discussions about him during the operation may become sufficiently upset to sue the anaesthetist. Patients are also somewhat
unceremoniously woken up by someone slapping their hands
and calling their name. This is rather different from the controlled way in which participants are awakened in a sleep laboratory when the contents of a REM dream are being logged.
Therefore anaesthetists do say that the lack of consciousness due
to anaesthesia is, at best, like NREM natural sleep.

Technically, this provides a way of getting the robot into deep,
stage 4, NREM sleep: reducing the generalisation of all the cells
in the system down to a minimum, as may be happening in a
deeply asleep living organism. This is akin to chemical control in
the brain that can influence large neural areas through a spread
of chemicals known as neurotransmitters. The reduction of generalisation need happen only for the requisite period of recuper-
ative time. What remains then is the need to ensure that the
thought automaton (axiom 2) finds the neutral states of its state
space as the generalisation of the cells is restored.

The landscapes and earthquakes of becoming awake

Neural network scientists think of all the states of a module as a
landscape full of holes in which the state of the module is imagined to be a ball. When the ball falls into a hole or a valley is analogous to having a meaningful thought. During waking life this
landscape is constantly being modified by sensory input. For
example if a tiger approaches at high speed, the landscape will
distort so as to make the 'flee' trough the largest and deepest at
that moment. The reduction of generalisation is like the flatten-
ing out of this landscape leaving the ball in a meaningless state.

But as the generalisation returns, the troughs return and the
ball will be drawn into a trough. This could be a recent thought
or, if the ball rolled arbitrarily far from a recently made trough, it
could be an older experience. There is also a trough that represents the desirable neutral state from which the thinking day
might begin. So how does one get the ball into the neutral state?
The answer is to have an earthquake to shake the ball out of the
undesirable state into the desirable one. The troughs of the land-

scape have mouths of different sizes and they have different depths. So the neutral state should have a large mouth and considerable depth. As said earlier, sensory input distorts the landscape of the thought module, therefore were the sensory input distorted in rapid arbitrary ways for short bursts, this would have the precise effect of the desired earthquake.

This may be exactly the role of the the pontine-geniculate-occipital (PGO) brain area in living organisms which was mentioned above. Then REM sleep and dreaming is due to the ball bouncing across the landscape and landing in a bizarre sequence of thoughts between shocks. Hopefully it will be in the neutral state on final awakening.

Complexity and sleep cycles

The thought landscape of a human being is enormously complex. Without going into the theoretical basis of this calculation an estimate may be that the human brain involves something of the order of the capacity of 10^{5000} (1 followed by 5000 zeros) distinguishable states. All this says is that the number is astronomically vast. Assuming that we have ten thought elements (such as 'pear' in 'I remember having a pear after dinner') every second of our waking lives, this would create only about 3×10^9 meaningful states among the vast number of possible meaningless ones. This complexity may explain the reason that there are several cycles between REM sleep and deeper NREM sleep as having just one go at reaching the neutral state may bring the ball closer to it but may not find it. Therefore evolution may have adapted the living system to have as many cycles of NREM to REM sleep as are necessary to achieve the final desired waking result. As this model is now getting a bit abstract and convoluted, a tangible simulated example may help to clarify things.

The dreaming automaton

Here I break away from the robot on a distant planet and will use an actual dream that occurred to me not so long ago. I was going to a concert at the Barbican Hall in London when I was stopped by a policeman on a motorbike who said that I had gone through a red traffic light a few streets back. I was incensed by this as, yes, the light had just gone amber as I crossed the intersection, but *red*, never! As might be expected, there was no arguing the point and I was in a hurry, so I accepted the fine notice the policeman handed me and heard him say that I could pay it within 30 days or else I would be summonsed to court. The Beethoven concert was wonderful and more than made up for the unpleasant encounter with the policeman. On getting home I was a bit annoyed that the light bulb in the kitchen had blown at I had to replace it before going to bed.

I awoke in the middle of the night from an obsessive dream in which the policeman had arrested the orchestra conductor and locked him up in my dark kitchen. This is a simplified version of the actual dream.

I shall simplify the experience and the dream even further to extract an explanation from the simulation. Using a digital neural simulator I put together two modules, a depictive, perceptual module (Axiom 1), and a 'thought' module (Axiom 2). I represented the day events in both modules as words :

> Being stopped by the police: POL (police), MON (money), CAR
> Beethoven performance: BET, CON (conductor)
> Lamp failure in the kitchen: LAM, KIT.
> There is also a neutral state which is all-white.

The complete state diagram of the thought automaton is shown in fig. 3.2

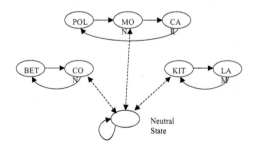

Figure 3.2: The waking state structure. The dotted arrows show changes which are less likely to occur while the solid ones indicate the available attractors.

As described above, in deep, stage 4 sleep when generalisation is at its lowest the diagram of fig. 3.2 disappears and the system wanders at random through its vast number of random states. Figure 3.3 is an actual recording of the states in the simulation of the thought module.

Sleep is assumed to proceed in cyclic stages: low generalisation (a) is the bottom of a cycle, with rising generalisation (b) and normal generalisation (c) is then accompanied in (d) by rising noise bursts in the depictive machinery. In (e), the noise bursts diminish as the system drifts towards being awake.

In the simulation, the noise bursts (representing PGO) were also applied to the state of the thought module to make the 'earthquake' really effective. However this may not always be necessary, it has to do with technical detail that is beyond the scope of this description.

Figure 3.3: Simulation of depictive and thought modules going from deep sleep (a) due to low generalisation, higher generalisation leading to NREM dream (b), REM sleep in one cycle (c), REM sleep in another cycle (d) and REM sleep entering the neutral state as the noise bursts diminish (e).

In low generalisation (a) both the depictive and the thought modules are in a non processing mode firing at random.

The notion of 'waking up the system' is an interesting one. It means that suddenly the depictive module is filled with waking sensory information. The system will 'remember' a dream by reporting whatever sustainable activity remains in the thought following this enforcement. (I shall comment on reporting bizarre dreams later.) Therefore (a) could be called deep NREM sleep (e.g. stage 3 or 4) in which, should the system be awakened, it would *not* report a coherent dream state. If awakened in (b), the system might report a very vague memory of a dream if this ghostly state is maintained or fall into some unrelated waking response to depictions in the perceptual module. Then in (c) and (d) the thought module falls into attractors in its state space (fig 3.2). This is an emergent REM sleep, as, were the system awakened, it is likely to remain in the last attractor which would be reported as a dream.

Why should eyes move? Of course, this model has no eyes, but, in more sophisticated models, eye movement is very much involved in the locking process that creates depictions in the thought module (see Chapter 2). It is likely that the attractors of such sophisticated models contain the muscular information that caused the locking. This may be stimulated during vivid dreaming. This means that the old notion of the system 'looking' at its dreams in REM sleep may actually be partly correct, but only in the sense that what looking took place in laying down the memory is associated with the memory itself. No *new* looking takes place according to this model.

Finally, as the system approaches a waking state and the level of noise in the noise bursts diminishes (e), there is a strong likelihood that the neutral state will be entered, achieving the task of waking up in a relaxed state from which new thinking and learning can take place.

Bizarre dreams

So far the model can only be seen as having dreams due to regular attractors in its state space. But this is not always the case. The bursts of noise can cause jumps such POL to CON to KIT, which roughly corresponds to my strange dream. A question is prompted by those who ask whether something is learned during REM sleep. The model strongly suggests that if a bizarre sequence occurs, for it to be remembered on waking it must, during sleep, have strengthened the links in state space between the elements that have been chained in a new way due to noise bursts.

Looking back at fig.3.2, for the sequence POL-CON-KIT to be sustained on sudden waking new links need to have been created between these states. New links mean that the dream has caused some changes in the functions of the cells, so the model indicates that learning must take place for bizarre dreams to be remembered.

Meaning of the model

Models of this kind serve two purposes: first, confirmation or denial of hypotheses of the behaviour of complex mechanisms and second, as design sketches for working systems such as a planetary exploration robot. The hypothesis supported by the above sleep model is that there exists a class of machines (of which the living brain may be one) which, to reduce the expenditure of energy, need to reduce the activity of their 'brains' without losing the state space trajectories that represent their lifetime experience. Such systems are characterised by having complex state structures and by needing neutral areas in their state spaces from which new thinking can start. So to avoid the problem of exiting from the energy-saving sleep into waking life and ending in an arbitrary thought pattern, a gradual process of arriving at the neutral state is needed. This skips over existing state structure causing the thought module to undergo experiences that could either be replays of recent experience or bizarre juxtapositions of previous memories. This class of organisms whether alive or constructed will, dream as a matter of necessity.

Whether the space exploring robot is best designed to be a member of this class of machines or not, is not clear. But as machine designers borrow more and more ideas from the excellent way that problems are solved in natural systems they also import some of the complexity of nature and then the design strategy implied by the model becomes a usable option.

The unconscious

As mentioned earlier, the concept of 'the unconscious' is inescapably linked to the ideas and practices of Sigmund Freud[3]. It implies that there is an area of thought that cannot be accessed during waking normal thought but nonetheless can influence waking life despite its inaccessibility. Such thoughts can, however, be accessed during dreams or possibly the induced sleep states of hypnosis.

In a fictional illustration, a psychoanalyst's client reports that he becomes deeply depressed particularly whenever his aging parents require his help from him. Attempts by the analyst to discuss childhood experiences fail and appear to deepen the depression. Then one day the patient arrives in a very disturbed state and wants to discuss a dream. He dreamt that his father had been murdered and that the murderer was his twin brother — but he did not have a twin brother. Gradually the analyst uses this link to uncover that the patient was harshly and unfairly treated by his father when he was young and harboured thoughts of killing his parent. But such thoughts were so awful that they were never accessed and were replaced by benign thoughts of concern for aging parents. While the dream fashioned the twin to accommodate this contradictory way of feeling about his father, it also created access to a previously unresolved feeling. The analyst could then proceed to get his patient to accept the awful truth of earlier feelings, and come to grips with current reality.

The depictive/axiomatic model and its behaviour during sleep can be extended to address physiological events that may have occurred in the above scenario, that is, the nature of the unconscious. It consists of state trajectories that have become disconnected from the normal waking state structure. The sketch in figure 3.4 is a highly simplified state space model of what may be going on. It is drawn in the style of figure 3.2 and

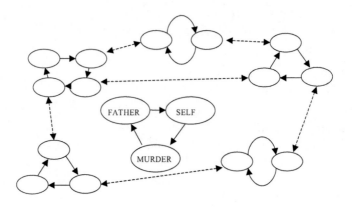

Figure 3.4: A thought state space showing an attractor that cannot be accessed from the other attractors (solid arrows) that are linked under waking conditions (dotted arrows) by appropriate sensory input.

shows no probable entry into an offending set of states. There could be many such inaccessible cycles that, because of their disconnected nature cannot truly be called attractors but would be sustained if entered by chance.

But, as we have seen in the above dream model, these isolated areas could be entered due to bursts of noise during REM sleep. In this case they could also be remembered as, it has been argued, links would be created to normal waking states during REM sleep. As a speculation it could be said that the psychoanalysis serves to get waking thought close to the hidden trajectory which increases the possibility of the linking dream taking place. At this point it is proper to ask why some such thought cycles *become* isolated.

Freud's notion of *repression* makes a lot of sense even at this technical level. The cultural environment in which we live defines that which can and that which cannot be thought about. Thinking about murdering one's father is a plan (recall Axiom 4) that is not culturally acceptable. The emotional evaluation (Axiom 5) is thoroughly negative (guilt, fear … etc.) and the plan is avoided. With time, any trajectory that approaches the plan is avoided and so links to the offending trajectory are lost. This is a technical way of saying that the thought is repressed. What is left are trajectories that carry the emotional baggage of guilt and fear but they are deflected into attractors such as the social desirability of having to care for parents. Help from an analyst (or an automata theoretician (!)) is needed.

Does this mean that as conscious machines are being designed, a new branch of psychoanalysis will need to be created: machine psychoanalysis? I do not think so. The thrust of this chapter has been to show that there is a theoretical way of understanding the effects of repressed thoughts. So maybe if our planetary robot gets into trouble due to unexplained emotions, all that earth control will have to do is to send an instruction to the machine to increase its noise bursts during periods of sleep.

Dreams and being conscious (again)

At the beginning of this chapter I raised a few questions about the importance of sleep and dreaming as part of the panoply of phenomena that go with being conscious. By way of a summary of this chapter we revisit these questions to see if progress has bee made.

What role do dreams have in affecting our waking consciousness? In terms of debates about the usefulness of dreams, they seem to be a necessary by-product of the journey between deep NREM sleep and being awake after a good sleep. The benefit from this is that stressful thoughts present when going to bed at night will be approached from more neutral ground in the morning. The stress may well return, but sleep and dreaming will have been involved in making waking life more tolerable. In cases of repressed unconscious thought, problematic inaccessible thoughts that leave the emotions in unresolved states can be accessed and perhaps resolved with the help of an expert.

Sleep, we have seen, may be necessary to prolong the life of both artificial and natural organisms. The cellular, attractor-laden structure of depictive systems requires careful control of the entry and exit into deep sleep, this implies global changes in cell generalisation and bursts of noise to stop the system from getting stuck in inappropriate attractors in the waking journey - this causes dreaming. These are the hypothesised cellular mechanisms that give rise to the dreaming model of this chapter.

So I am suggesting that dreams are not whimsical, on the contrary, they are indicative of the way brain mechanisms function. They are also not a continuation of the dualist notion of the mind in the sense that they are not a mystical, unexplained link to the future or to divinity. There is nothing in dreams for anyone trying to argue that internal sensation is distinct from the working of depictive cellular mechanisms.

Chapter 4

The Octopus with a Stomach Ache

Are animals conscious?

In the early 1990s, I was happy to have been Catherine Myers' PhD adviser. She developed a fascination for the way that an octopus avoids getting ill from eating less than desirable little crabs. Were it just a case of avoiding crabs with special markings, this would not be too strange a tale to tell. After all, most animals learn to avoid unpleasant experiences by using their visual discrimination and reacting to it. The remarkable part of the story is that it takes a fair length of time for the octopus to digest this crab and become ill. In the meantime it may have eaten other crabs with other markings all of which are perfectly fine. So how does he learn which among that batch is the crab to avoid in the future?

This type of experience acquisition is technically known as 're-inforcement learning' and Dr. Myers did a wonderful job of exploring the way that the neural networks of the octopus, or, indeed neural networks in general, could learn in this fashion. This works by the neural network assigning temporary 'stomach ache' values to the markings of crabs eaten over a given recent period of time. Those that occur often in this list have their danger labels 'reinforced' so the rogue crabs are eventually identified. In thinking about this and the five axioms of being conscious, it becomes evident that reinforcement learning contains an intricate interaction between axiom 1, perceiving crabs, axiom 2, memory and axiom 5, having appropriate feelings about perceived crabs.

The octopus appears to be even more intelligent than just guarding against stomach aches. A friend in Greece, Anthony Mathielis, an expert octopus hunter, told me an even more amazing story. Some species of octopus will observe the opening of a clam shell and drop a little stone into it so that the clam cannot shut again. This makes it easy for the octopus to gobble up the clam meat at its leisure. Is this an example of the presence of planning machinery of the axiom 4 kind, or could it be explained as some unthinking automatic reaction by a largely unconscious animal? Which leads me to the main point of this chapter. Are these curious feats just automatic, albeit complex, reactions of the animal to their environment or is this evidence of some conscious contemplation?

The broader question

Are non-human animals conscious or do they just slavishly follow in-built or boringly learned rules? There seems to be a vast difference of opinion between individuals on this, a difference of opinion that gets to the very roots of what it is to be conscious. Some say that animals are unthinking automata. Others tell us that they are as emotional and sensitive as we are. What experiments can be done to distinguish between the two? I wish to get into these debates to see whether the axiomatic ideas discussed in chapter 2 help in deciding who is right.

The discussion about whether animals are conscious or not is fraught with pitfalls. For example, the reason that we readily accept that all humans around us are conscious is because they will not deny it. Of course they could be lying and really be precisely those zombies that David Chalmers argues might be logically possible (see Chapter 7). On the whole, however, I have no reason to believe that other humans feel about themselves differently from what I feel about me. Within the limits of language, other humans are capable of telling me what it is like for them to be conscious and that feels familiar. So why is the argument different for animals? They cannot speak, so this might be one reason it becomes only too easy to deny that they are conscious. So while it is not so difficult to know what it might be like to be Fred, a person with whom I have just been chatting in a pub, it is much harder to imagine what it is like to be the proverbial Nagel bat. So does this make it less likely for a bat to be conscious or do I have to think more carefully about the role of language in assessments of whether an organism is conscious or not?

There is also the opposite effect. Some find it only too easy to attribute consciousness to their pets or even their cars. It is not unusual to hear, 'Of course my Fido is conscious – look at the way he is pleased to see me!' Or even, 'The car is being stubborn this morning – it refuses to start.' Our preparedness to attribute consciousness to objects should not be confused with evidence that they are. In fact, gathering evidence of whether animals are conscious or not is astoundingly difficult. Some philosophers might even argue that it is impossible as behaviour, they argue, is not an indication of consciousness. Nevertheless there is a dedicated group of people in many academic Biology and Zoology departments who are trying to gather this evidence in the principled traditions of science. There are excellent texts on this research which I shall try to summarise here and look at from the perspective of the five axioms. Particularly recommended is Marian Stamp Dawkins' *Through Our Eyes Only: The Search For Animal Consciousness*[1] and Donald Griffin's *Animal Minds*.[2]

A mini comment on the neural correlates of consciousness

A number of neurologists who are looking for the 'neural correlates of consciousness' in human beings, Crick and Koch[3] for example, obtain their data from experiments done on monkeys or cats. In this field of work there is the tacit assumption that the brains of animals generate consciousness for animals in much the same way as the human brain does this for humans.

[1] Stamp Dawkins, M. (1998), *Through Our Eyes Only: The Search for Animal Consciousness* (Oxford University Press).
[2] Griffin, D. (1992), *Animal Minds* (University of Chicago Press).
[3] Crick, F. and Koch, C. (1998), 'Consciousness and neuroscience', *Cereb Cortex*, **8** (2), 97–107.

It is also possible to anticipate that taking the axiomatic point of view will reveal that most mammals have such axiomatic mechanisms in place that potentially can generate consciousness for them in the same way as they do it for me. But this will be better argued as the whole story of what is known about animal minds is told.

Not all animals are stubborn mules

Our language is peppered with expressions that create a division between 'clever' people and 'stupid' animals: 'learning parrot fashion'; 'a silly ass'; 'a dumb beast' and so on. In technical language this implies that animal responses to their environments and other animals are in some way simple and, in particular, do not involve the kind of conscious thought that I use in my daily life. In contrast to this, much of the science of animal consciousness is directed at showing that many animals have a great deal more than direct, reactive responses to what is in front of them.

The story of the clam-baiting octopus is one example of the way that an opening clam acts as a stimulus which leads to a complex sequence of actions in the animal that achieves the result of jamming the clam and satisfying his own hunger. Is this a sign of conscious contemplation or following some innate rule? Not an easy question. In robotics, the task could also be accomplished in two ways. First, using the programming methods of artificial intelligence, one could build a robot that follows the built-in rule:

> If the clam is opening, then pick up a stone and drop it into the shell.

In a robot such a rule could come from a programmer and, according to the principles of this book there would be no consciousness involved as there would be no depictive, axiom. 1, activity in this process. In a non-human animal, to explain this kind of automaticity, 'evolution' is the scapegoat in the explanation. For some reason it is often believed that, in animals, evolved rules cut out consciousness.

On the other hand, the robot could have an axiomatic set of mechanisms which, having seen another robot perform this trick (axiom 1 — Out-There Perception), builds that experience into an axiom 2 dynamic neural system(imagination and memory). By all the arguments used in this book, it would be hard to deny that the robot is, on the way to being conscious, depending on the degree of presence of the other axiomatic mechanisms. I would say that in an animal, discovery of such brain action perhaps would also make it hard to deny that in its own way, it too is conscious.

Before unpacking the way in which it may be possible to check to what extent these hypotheses are applicable, we consider some other examples that Marian Dawkins has highlighted. For the time being, in thinking of these examples, we bear in mind that *both* the purely reactive as well as the axiomatic mechanisms require an equal and fair consideration. Quite a lot is at stake: the axiomatic mechanisms suggest inner depiction which may be central to conscious human-like deliberation while the reactive one does not.

The first line of attack by those who argue that animals are not conscious is to say that their behaviour is somehow 'simple' in comparison to humans. Humans think ahead, they say, and plan their behaviour in subtle and projected ways. Animals at best appear to react to their environment and other animals in rather direct ways. Human planning requires conscious deliberation, they add, while animal reaction does not. The clam-baiting octopus seems to support a counter argument to this assumption. It is not a simple reaction — it may be copied from peers and remembered. Indeed Marion Dawkins presents many other examples that seriously undermine this 'simplicity' argument. Of course the complexity of the clam baiting behaviour is not a *guarantee* of conscious contemplation, but, at least, it does not slam the door on the possibility as does the simplicity argument.

Marsh tits are good at Pelmanism

Taking two examples from Dawkins' catalogue, the first draws attention to the precision with which some birds remember where they have hidden food in trees. David Sherry[4] of Toronto pushed this ability to the limit by working with artificial trees that had holes in which food could be hidden. In one of his experiments he used 72 holes of which 15 contained peanuts. He made the task difficult for the European marsh tits he was using for the experiment and allowed them to see the food but not touch it. It was covered in Perspex! The birds were removed, the holes opened but then covered with little Velcro-secured doors. Then, 24 hours later, the birds were allowed back and tracked. They did not waste their time with the empty holes and picked open the doors where the food was hidden. This is a prodigious feat of memory reminiscent of that game of cards called 'Pelmanism'. A pack of cards is scattered face down on a surface. Each player turns over two cards. If they match as, for example, two Kings or two sevens, the player removes them from the table and adds them to his winnings. The player who collects most cards wins. So as play progresses, each player begins to know where the cards are and things get easier as the number of cards on the table is reduced . But the marsh tits seem far better at this task than we are.

However, a cold, scientific assessment of the behaviour of birds would say that this is a memory act which a programmed computer could perform even better (it would have perfect memory). Therefore we judge that no consciousness may be involved. But then, when *I* introspect on the way that *I* play Pelmanism, I suspect that no computer-like storage of data is going on. The movement of my eyes and head over the cards is involved in generating the positional, muscular data that that creates for me an imagined picture of what is hidden and this is then lodged in the depictive memory which inspires my actions. The mechanisms of axioms 1 and 2 are hard at work, while atten-tion (axiom 3) and planning (axiom 4) are present. The pleasure I have in knowing and predicting what a card may hide suggests that even Axiom 5 mechanisms are at work. Bearing in mind the structure of the brain of a marsh tit suggests that mechanisms

[4]   Sherry, D.F. (1984), 'Food storage, memory and marsh tits', *Animal Behaviour*, **32**, 451–464.

more like my axiomatic ones are at work rather that those that drive my PC. One might even say that nature abhors computer architectures and favours axiomatic/depictive structures. So while this example does not provide hard evidence that the marsh tit is conscious, it points to the possibility that it is, without giving unequivocal support to the notion that the bird operates in an automatic computer-like way.

The altruistic vampire bat

The second striking example of complex behavious is that of vampire bats and their feeding habits.[5] They leave their cave and hopefully find a cow or a horse to feed from. They drink the blood but are also capable of storing it to feed others. While feeding members of their own family could be seen as being automatic and 'instinctive', they actually feed others in the cave who particularly need it. The surprising result is that the beneficiaries of such generosity, on other occasions return the favour. They will single out bats who were kind to them and feed them as a matter of priority.

This is not simple reactive behaviour. Even a model that does not involve consciousness would need elements of subtle memory, recognition and classification of individual bats and some planning algorithm to decide which bat should be fed first. Were the model to be axiomatic and depictive, that is, supportive of the organism being conscious, all five axioms would be at work: perception to position self in a colony of known bats; imagination to recall the kindness of other bats; attention to control a search among bats in the bat cave and emotion to evaluate the several plans related to feeding different bats and creating an order of priority.

Again, the complex behaviour of the bat does not provide evidence as to which of these models is the more appropriate, but, because the bat brain shares architectural features with other living organisms known to be conscious (me, for a start) the observed behaviour leaves open the possibility that the bat

---

[5]   Wilkinson, G.S. (1984), 'Reciprocal food sharing in the vampire bat', *Nature*, **308**, 181–184.

might be conscious. Indeed, as in the last case one might even lean towards favouring the axiomatic model.

Clever Hans and other good acts

Marion Dawkins goes to much trouble to point out that it is possible to read too much into some seemingly complex behaviour in animals which then turns out to be a great deal simpler than at first appeared. The horse that does sums, the dog that speaks and the chimpanzee that uses deaf signing language have all been quoted as examples of some kind of 'human-like' thought in animals if not direct evidence of consciousness.

But, as Dawkins points out, the attribution of thought may be a complex explanation where there might be simpler ones. Clever Hans was a horse in a show act of the early 1900s where the animal was shown to do arithmetic by responding to questions such as 'what is 5+4 ?' by stamping its foot nine times. Impressive as this was, it turned out that the horse would get it wrong or not even attempt to answer if someone other than the owner asked the question and was present during the stamping. This is not a direct accusation of cheating just a suggestion that the horse was responding to some barely perceptible reaction of the owner. So starting with the question asked in a particular tone by a particular person, the horse learned that he must start stamping. When the right number is reached the horse might have noticed a tiny change in posture or facial expression in the owner of which even the owner may not have been conscious. This simple reactive behaviour would not need axiomatic mechanisms and is not good evidence for their presence.

There are several examples of chimpanzees learning language by naming things or asking for things with sign language or selection and movement of symbols magnetically attached to a metallic board. But, as Dawkins points out, the presence and influence of the human trainer during the performance of these acts appears to be a necessary part of the act. What this indicates is that the explanation lies in the superb and unexpected ability in the chimpanzees to react to body language, facial expression and involuntary sounds generated by the trainer. British magician and Psychologist, Richard Wiseman once told me that he is investigating a similar ability in some magicians. These performers have trained themselves to read facial and bodily signs that indicate some of what a person is thinking to the magician but is imperceptible to anyone else. They would then present this as a feat of 'mind reading'. Of course, this does not mean that some thought is not going on in the chimpanzee, it merely stresses that the simple mechanistic reaction has not been ruled out. According to the arguments of this book, the feats can be performed without the presence of the axiomatic processes of being conscious.

When is behaviour inescapably thoughtful?

Even in the absence of human trainers, animals are capable of the most complex tasks to which 'thought' may be attributed by a human observer. The well known dance of the scout bee that indicates to other bees in the hive the direction and distance of pollen-rich flowers, is often described as an example of thoughtful activity. But this too could be achieved with non-axiomatic mechanisms. It is what computer scientists call 'scheduling'. That is, given a particular state of input data, the machine can be programmed to react with a complex, but memorised, sequence. There need be no axiom 1 sensation of being an entity in a world, no axiom 2 memory of such experience. There may be axiom 3 attentional mechanisms at work in searching out the food, but not much of evaluation of alternative plans (axioms 4 and 5).

So, are there signs of the presence of such axiomatic mechanisms that might be evident in the complex behaviour of animals? Dawkins argues that such proof might come from the ability of an animal to do something new, which depends on having to 'reconfigure in its mind' a previously learned behaviour. In robot terms this means that having been taught, say, to go down a corridor and turning left at the third door on the left, the robot can, in response to some request, reconfigure its plan to enter a door it has never been taught to enter. In other words, axiom 4 planning mechanisms must tell the robot that it can, via an imagined axiom 2 event do the required task. How much evidence is there for such reconfiguration and flexibility in animal studies? Again we borrow some case studies identified by Marion Dawkins to see whether there is evidence of axiomatic activity.

The clock-watching pigeon

Can evidence be found in animals that there is some imaginative prediction at work which could be due to axiom 2 mechanisms? Marion Dawkins highlights an experiment performed by Neiworth and Rilling,[6] who tested pigeons to see if they could 'think of' the evolution of a simple progression in time. The pigeons were shown a dial similar to a clock face with a single hand that rotates at a steady speed. As this was displayed on a computer screen, the hand could be made to disappear and reappear in any position at the experimenter's will. Pigeons were shown the hand moving, disappearing and reappearing. They were rewarded if they pecked at a gate when the hand reappeared where it should have been had it continued steadily during its disappearance, and not rewarded if the hand appeared in an arbitrary position.

On the whole, pigeons were good at learning this task. As care was taken to make sure that the hand reappeared in the right position, but not in a position that might have been used in a learning trial, the experiment demonstrated that the pigeon applied a general thought process in a situation new to it. Were a robot to be designed to do the same thing, one thing becomes blindingly clear. This cannot be done with a simple rule of the form:

> If sensory input X occurs, then peck' because X can be any point on the dial.

The kind of rule that describes the bird's behaviour is:

> If sensory input X occurs *and* the inner mechanism is in some state Y (where Y predicts X) then peck.

---

[6]   Rilling, M.E. and Neiworth J.J. (1991), 'How animals use images', *Sci Prog.*, **75** (298 Pt 3–4), 439–452.

This means that there must be an inner representation that is continually anticipating the correct Y and expected X. Interestingly if this representation is 'depictive' then Y is some form of depiction of the expected X. That is, depiction means that the bird is visualising where the hand should be at any moment of its disappearance. Of course, some other inner representation might be at work: the experiment does not tell us that the representation is depictive, but it does not cut out this possibility. Indeed, a depictive representation in a robot would be the easiest way of solving this problem, as the comparison between the inner state and the perceived external event could easily be achieved with some kind of image comparator.

It would be very difficult to maintain that the bird is *not* thinking in some way if 'thought' is an inner activity which is not directly driven by sensory input. In this case the input is a missing clock hand and it is an inner activity that allows the pigeon to solve the problem . But the passage of time is a rather specific form of 'thought' involving a mix of conscious and unconscious processes. In needs a little more explanation.

The passage of time

What is it to 'be conscious' of the passage of time? I know that during waking time, I can roughly predict what my watch will say before I actually look at it. But I cannot say that I am depictively conscious of the moving hands of a clock all my waking hours. This implies that my brain registers neurally the passage of time without this necessarily being in my depicted consciousness. How can this work? How can I be conscious and not conscious of the passage of time simultaneously? Neurological studies, particularly those carried out by Deborah Harrington of the University of New Mexico, Albuquerque, reveal the implication of several brain areas in the perception of time,[7] but these are not localised. There is no clock in the brain, but several areas like the basal ganglia (well known as the villains of Parkin-

---

[7] Harrington, D.L. and Haaland, K.Y. (1999), 'Neural underpinnings of temporal processing: A review of focal lesion, pharmacological and functional imaging research', *Rev. Neurosci.*, **10** (2), 91–116.

son's disease), the cerebellum (the low lump at the back of the head) and the 'middle-frontal' and 'inferior-parietal' cortices, if damaged, show up as deficits in the perception of the passage of time.

So when I predict the time before looking at my watch, this is likely to involve attention to a whole lot of otherwise *unconscious* time processing mechanisms (axiom 3) which are then translated into an imagined vision (axiom 2) of the hands of my watch. Does this conscious/unconscious cooperation exist in pigeons? Experiments seem to point in that direction as a small but significant piece in the jigsaw puzzle suggesting that animals are conscious.

Order

In our daily lives we are continuously expecting events in the world to occur in a particular order. At traffic lights for example, if stopping for the red light, our thinking leads us to expect the lights to turn to green before long. Or, if we approach green lights, we are wary of the fact that they might change to amber and then to red. So we are conscious of an order in which the light events happen in the world. In short, thinking of events that occur in a particular order is a fundamental element of being conscious. Someone not capable of such thought would be said to have a thought disorder, that is, a deficit of consciousness.

In an attempts to discover whether thinking about order occurs in animals, Herb Terrace[8] set up an experiment not dissimilar from the traffic light example above. Differently coloured lights could appear in a line in eight positions. He rewarded pigeons for pecking in a specific order at three different colours (say, green→red→blue) irrespectively of where they appeared in the eight possible positions. They learned to do this and showed that they were not deterred by new positions or distracting, unfamiliar lights. The pigeon's ability to adapt to new situations was checked — they learned new sequences similar to old ones more easily than dissimilar ones, suggesting that input

[8]   Terrace, H.S. (1991), 'Chunking during serial learning by a pigeon: I. Basic evidence', *J Exp Psychol Anim Behav Process.*, Jan, **17** (1), 81–93.

is being related to remembered sequences. Again, the evidence points to 'thought' as a feature of being conscious, as possibly being present in the animal, but this must be treated with care.

Sequence thinking?

Suggestions that being sensitive to order implies the presence of thought, needs close scrutiny. We recall that a simple neural net in which the output of the neurons feed back to the inputs of others (called a dynamic or recursive neural net), is capable of learning to become sensitive to sequences. This is because the inner patterns on the feedback connections can have a chaining character — one state leads to another. This kind of system can be responsible for endowing an animal with the ability to peck at lights in the right order. But could such a network be said to be 'thinking about order'. Yet again, the use of words threatens to derail the sense of the argument. When I think about the way that traffic lights change, this *is* likely to be due to some neural net with feedback at work in my brain. In fact, this is the mechanism that underpins imagination in Axiom 2. But a lot else may be going on in my mind: is the radio telling me important things about the traffic and am I late for my appointment? So when I refer to my own thinking, this seems to point to a much richer experience than might be needed by the pigeon pecking at lights in the right order. This may explain why we feel uneasy at the suggestion that order picking *alone* implies thought. Still, a great deal more evidence is required to satisfy the sceptic that the order picking pigeon is conscious. But again, it is important to note that the evidence points in the direction of the proposition of the presence of consciousness rather than against it.

Of mice and tunnels

Like the astute sleuth in a detective thriller, the animal consciousness scientist tries to create increasingly revealing experimental traps that provide evidence for their suspicions of the presence of consciousness. Canadian scientist Hank Davis is particularly interested in whether animals can have a sense of number.[9] This is not the doubtful counting ability of Clever Hans seen earlier in this chapter. Rather it is the fact that a conscious appreciation of number adds flexibility to the way that an organism makes decisions in a complex world. I may describe the position of my house as the third on the left after the corner. However when I come home in the evening, I automatically sense this third position without having to count. So this is somewhat different from appreciating numbers in the sense that they represent quantity (a three-egg omelette is bigger than a two-egg omelette) or arithmetical functions (three times two is six).

Hank Davis with his student Sheree-Ann Bradford, devised an experiment where a memory of the positional meaning of number was essential in helping rats to find food rewards. They designed free-standing tunnels that could be positioned perpendicularly to the walls of a large box. To avoid smell clues they all contained food, but for all except one the food was blocked off with the blockage hidden behind a pair of swing gates. All the tunnels had swing doors. Six tunnels were used and in the first experiment, the tunnels were lined up against the wall to the left of the entrance. Rats were divided into three groups, the first found food in the fourth tunnel from the entrance, the second in the fifth and the third in the sixth. The rats mastered the finding of their appointed tunnel, and were neither perturbed by changes in the spacing between the tunnels nor if the line of tunnels was distorted to have the last three at right angles to the first three. Conclusion? The sought numerical/positional representation exists within the rat. Snag? As usual, how indicative is this feat of the presence of conscious, positional 'thought'?

Re-phrasing the question, we are asking whether the rat entering the tunnel box is simply producing an automatic response to environmental input with no mental depiction of what it has learned, or whether its actions are determined by depiction and decisions based on internal thoughts. For the first to work, the rat would have to have a logic where the environment as projected into the visual system triggers actions directly. But the

[9]   Davies, H. and Bradford, S.A. (1987), 'Counting behaviour in rats in a simulated natural environment', *Ethology*, **73**, 265–280.

variations in the experiment (tunnel spacing, tunnel orientation) suggest that the environmental cues are different from the ones for which an exact response was learned. and despite this, the mouse finds its rewards.

A simple way of explaining this using axiomatic theory is to evoke attentional (axiom 3) mechanisms where the mouse has learned to attend to the appropriate tunnel by scanning its view past the earlier inappropriate ones. So there appears to be strong evidence of the presence of attentional axiom (3) mechanisms and considerable evidence for the presence of an internal representation (axiom 2) which, when internally attended, generates the plan (axiom 4) for identifying the appropriate tunnel. There may also be a need for a weak evaluation of the plan that anticipates pleasure on seeing the appropriate tunnel (axiom 5). So a strange thing has happened. What from the outside can be interpreted as a counting ability, is driven internally by a mix of a depiction and an internal attentional scan of this. There need not be an explicit representation of number. This suggests that humans through the use of symbols have abstracted this combination of inner representation and attention to create the concept of number. But does this say that humans are conscious and animals are not?

It surely does not. Just taking the case of humans who have not been able to develop a useful language, one would not begin to think that they are not conscious. The case of Caspar Hauser comes to mind — brought up in the wild without language, few would argue that he was not conscious because he did not use language.[10] It seems vital not to confuse consciousness with knowledge and experience, otherwise a university professor would be seen as being more conscious than one of her first year students.

Emotion in animals

Another effect of a developed language among human beings is that they can communicate their emotional states to others. When someone says 'I am angry' or 'I am happy', we know what

---

[10]   Wassermann, J. (1985), *Caspar Hauser* (New York: Carroll & Graf).

it's like for the speaker to be angry or happy. Using axiom 2 machinery we can imagine what it's like to be in the position of the person that is expressing their emotion. This is also axiom 5 machinery at work. If John's wallet has been stolen, I can imagine the same thing happening to me, so that when John expresses his anger at what has happened, I replicate in my imagination what he may be feeling. In humans, inferring (rightly or wrongly) the state of other minds is sometimes hailed as the pinnacle of being conscious. This also makes it difficult to work out the emotional states of animals. While we can observe their anguish or pleasure at times, we just cannot work out what it's like for them because we are highly aware of the fact that their existence is somewhat different from ours. The life, habits and needs even of species close to ours, like a chimpanzee, are sufficiently different from ours to make 'putting ourselves in their place' highly limited. And then they cannot tell us about their inner states.

Of course, as said earlier we sometimes easily attribute emotions such as anger, fear or surprise to dogs, cats and even bees. The reason that this is seen as not being 'scientific', I suspect, is due to the lack of evidence that an animal can *imagine* itself into situations that are mediated by emotion. That is, the interaction between axiom 4 and 5 which, in ourselves provides 'feelings' about futures we are predicting for ourselves needs to be proven before we can start believing in animal consciousness. Marian Dawkins (p. 160) is quite explicit about this:

> In asking whether animals have emotions, we may have established that in some way they do as we do but we have not yet answered the critical question of whether they feel as we feel.

Noting the somewhat pessimistic tone in which Dawkins separates the way that behaviour provides evidence which does not point to sensation, I wish to argue that from the axiomatic/depictive perspective, the pessimism could be relieved. Among the most advanced consciousness-seeking experiments on which Dawkins reports, there are tests with both hens and pigs where the animals were faced with choices, all of which were known to be desirable in isolation: reaching comfortable places to be, finding food or congregating with other animals. The tests measured the effort that the animals were prepared to exert in order to achieve a goal. For example the two goals of a hen may be to go to a comfortable place where food was available or join a crowd of other hens for the purpose of being in company. In single task experiments it had been shown that the animal would take action to achieve either of these goals that was on offer. With two tasks, the effort was measured by noting how many small gaps the animal was prepared to squeeze through to achieve its goal. The result? Hens just prefer food and comfort to being with other hens. Similarly pigs prefer food to the company of other pigs.

This ability to make choices and 'prefer' end goals points to an axiom 4 activity of 'planning' ahead and evaluating the imagined outcome using an 'emotion' in the sense of axiom 5. Of course, axiom 2 is implicated in 'imagining' the outcome of a planned action, and 1 and 3 are at work all the time. So there we have it - even though one could imagine some reactive rules that could model the way animals make their choices, this seems to be increasingly less plausible as the possible behaviour of axiomatic depictive mechanisms fits the measured data.

Centrally, if axiomatic/depictive machinery is responsible for my conscious emotions, it is very likely that a monkey with an anatomy very similar to mine should have similar machinery for making its choices and that this should include emotions of which the animal is conscious. Why should a monkey's brain anatomy be reactive and unconscious when my very similar anatomy is said to account for my sense of being conscious?

Why should animals **not** be conscious?

One must surely admire the persistence with which scientists like Marian Dawkins pursue animal minds in the face of that huge philosophical hurdle that other minds are only accessible through imagined projections of ourselves into others. Dawkins summarises her philosophy as follows (p.178):

> ... [when] we are left with a hard core of studies that make it extremely likely that at least some animals think in rudimentary

ways and that they experience pleasure and suffering sufficiently for these to matter to them, then it seems positively
unscientific *not* to consider the possibility that we are looking at
the outward and visible signs of inner conscious awareness.
Scientific evidence as well as common sense now demand that
we take the step of inferring consciousness in species other than
our own.

The theme of this chapter has been to underscore a similar philosophy: what could lead us to assume that animals are *not* conscious, not due to their behaviour but given that they have brain
anatomies to some extent similar to ours. They are likely to have
axiomatic mechanisms, so what would stop these from working
properly? We pursue two propositions that argue *against* animal
consciousness.

> **Proposition 1**. Animal brains do not make the animal conscious
> because they *react* to sensory input without 'thinking' about it.
> That is, animal brains simply transform input into behaviour.

It is clearly difficult for experimenters to dispel this notion for
the following simple reason. The experiments usually test a
rather narrow ability. The European marsh tit's memory is being
tested in one experiment while the rat's sense of number is at
stake in another. Whatever the competence of the animal in one
of these areas, it is not too difficult to think of a reactive rather
than contemplative mechanism that performs the task. Were I to
be tested for my Pelmanism prowess, we have already said that
this could be replicated by a rather simple computer that trans-
lates input into action. But, taking the introspective stance, I
know that my actions while playing Pelmanism are not automatic and purely reactive. I use my sense of perception (Ax 1)
mental imagery (Ax 2), some attention (Ax 3), perhaps not much
planning (Ax 4) and emotion only after the action (Ax 5): elation
at finding the card and misery at failing so to do. I would not say
that I was unconscious during the task.

Now comes the argument that seems to come to me repeat-
edly: If the marsh tit's brain has evolved in much the same way
as mine, that is, as a neural, multi-module architecture, the difference between the two is one of scale but not necessarily one of
principle. There is no theoretical reason known which says that

you need to have a brain of a certain size for the smooth functioning of axiomatic mechanisms to cut in. The upshot of this is that
the axiomatic way is the natural way for evolving living organisms to acquire their processing ability. So, to counteract proposition 1 and put the argument in a balanced way, equal credence
must be given to the idea that consciousness comes with the neurological territory of brains in all organisms that possess brains
rather than calling for the evolution of special non-axiomatic
brains for animals. What I am saying is that consciousness
through axiomatic processes may be the simplest way of brains
to grow to meet the needs of the organism that houses them. It is
our culture that requires that we believe that we humans are
unreachably complex and important. It is our vanity that
requires that we imagine that something that we possess cannot
be possessed by the rat or the marsh tit.

> **Proposition 2**. Animals are not conscious as they cannot reason
> about their own consciousness.

Yes humans do reason about their own consciousness, but what
does this mean? Primarily it means that humans can talk about
their inner sensations and even wonder where they came from.
But this is not a prerequisite for being conscious. It's the other
way around: consciousness is a pre-requisite for discussion.
Human reasoning is a consequence of two things: being conscious and having a highly expressive language. It is known
from the pioneering observations of bees by Karl von Frish[11]
where he discovered that the foraging bee returning to its nest
will only dance if other 'unloader' bees 'tell it if the food it
brought back is of good quality'. That is, the unloaders assess the
food and decide whether they are satisfied with its quality and
communicate their decision . Of course all this could be said in
talk that disallows the possibility of bees being conscious: 'the
unloaders react automatically to identify the quality of the food
and behave in such a way that causes the forager to dance, also
automatically'. The latter may strike one as being slightly
contrived.

---

[11] von Frisch, K. (1967), *The Dance Language and Orientation of Bees*
(Cambridge, MA: Harvard University Press).

Of course, the bees are not conversing about the nature of their consciousness, but they may be communicating that of which they are conscious. The difference in humans is that the richness of language allows us not only to communicate the content of our consciousness but also to ponder what it could be that allows us to be conscious. This is a factor that arises from 'content' arguments rather than the factors that make us conscious. Many people may never have pondered about what it is that makes them conscious which does not mean that they are not conscious.

Content

The last few points above need amplification. One of the major misapprehensions in discussions of whether animals are conscious or not is the idea that some factor is missing or present that engenders consciousness in this group of living things and not in others. This needs to be replaced by the question: 'of *what* can an organism be conscious?' The key factor that might explain the observable difference between the conscious life of a bat and that of a human being is that their respective mechanisms, despite possibly having depictive/axiomatic processes in common, afford them a very different access to sensation. Humans are lucky, they have a highly developed brain that has allowed language to emerge. It would be a gross mistake to argue that organisms that cannot be conscious of, say, the poverty of the people of Somalia are not conscious at all. As we have seen, the vampire bat, affected by the need of another bat in the same nest, with its axiomatic/depictive brain, is likely to be fully conscious of things that are important to *its* life and that of its peers. Poverty in Somalia is relevant to ours and that of our peers.

What transpires from the discussion in this chapter is that the presence of consciousness in animals is made likely through the similarities between animal and human brains, which contrasts with the notion that animal brains are like simple reactive computational mechanisms. However the presence of axiomatic mechanisms does not determine how extensive this consciousness is. An important theory which suggests that animals only have a reduced primary consciousness where humans have a 'higher' faculty needs to be briefly considered.

Higher order thought: ethical implications?

One of the arguments as to whether animals are or are not conscious concerns the idea of Higher Order Thought (HOT). Some philosophers believe that a mental state cannot 'be conscious' unless it is accompanied by a thought that recognises that one *is* in that state.[12] In other words I am conscious only if I feel 'I am conscious of being conscious'. Does an animal that is perceiving or remembering a tree conceptualise about itself being in that state? HOT proponents argue that an animal has no *need* to think about being conscious, and therefore is not fully conscious. Yes, it might have the internal states suggested in the studies reported in this chapter, but this extra layer of thinking about thinking is missing.

The fact that while animals might feel pain but are not conscious of feeling pain has led to a debate as to whether sympathy for animal suffering can be attenuated, strongly affecting the moral stance that humans might have towards animals. Peter Carruthers, professor of philosophy at the University of Maryland,[13] while embracing the notion that very few non-human animals would have the ability to conceptualise 'about' their mental states, argues that this should not diminish the respect that people have for animals. This should stem from sympathy for the frustration of basic (low order) desires. In other words he argues that the primary fact that animals may feel pain is sufficient for us to have the required sympathy, even if somehow we believe that they are not fully conscious.

I am somewhat sceptical about the need for a HOT theory of consciousness for the following simple reason. It either implies the existence of some form of separate mechanism that is superimposed on those required for primary consciousness, or it is

---

[12] Rosenthal, D. (1993), 'Thinking that one thinks'. In M. Davies and G. Humphreys (eds.), *Consciousness* (Oxford, Blackwell), pp. 197–223.
[13] Carruthers, P. (2000), *Phenomenal Consciousness: A Naturalist Theory* (Cambridge University Press).

some sort of additional behaviour mode of the same mechanisms that produce primary consciousness. It is doubtful that the former can be supported by neuroanatomy while the second is just another thought and is explained by primary mechanisms. David Rosenthal,[14] a leading proponent of HOT, has reported that MRI investigations have shown some additional activity in the medial frontal cortex when participants are asked to think about their mental states. This requires a great deal more experimentation. From the axiomatic/depictive point of view, a Higher Order Thought (gee, I am conscious of seeing a green apple) is just another thought like a decision to buy apples at the market (gee, this green apple looks good enough to eat) or awareness of the implications of a newspaper article (gee, the Democrats have chosen their candidate for the Presidency). In other words, this too should be considered as a content issue as mentioned in the last section. Not all conscious organisms have the same capacity for sophisticated thought. People invent ideas like HOT, animals, indeed, have no need to do so. But this does not imply that an animal is not conscious of dangers and threats to its life in much the same way that we are. It seems to me that evoking HOT in humans refers to a competent mode of thinking a bit like the ability to do arithmetic or to play chess, but it is not a mode that qualifies consciousness.

Summary

We have seen interesting examples of complex behaviours in animals, behaviours that strongly suggest that inner mental states are present. The difficulty lies with the philosophical problem of third-party access to first party sensations. I have suggested that looking just at the way that brains have evolved and achieve their properties, is it likely that axiomatic mechanisms are present in animals and not only the human variety. But while this does not mean that we are all conscious of the same thing (the content question) it does mean that it is hard to deny animals the consciousness that they need to exist in a complex world.

[14] Rosenthal, D. (2002), 'The HOT model of consciousness'. In Rita Carter, *Consciousness* (London: Weidenfeld and Nicolson).

Chapter 5

The Missing
Gorilla

Is consciousness an illusion?

There are some wonderful films doing the rounds of neuroscience and consciousness conferences that cause amazement and surprise the first time they are seen. One by Simons and Chabris (1999)[1] shows a group of people bouncing ball between them. The audience are asked to count the number of times a particular person bounces the ball. The astonishing event is that a person in a gorilla suit walks across the playing area, but only about 20% of the observers actually notice it. When shown the film again and released from the counting task, the audience shriek with laughter and disbelief. Some even swear that the film has been changed.

Another amusing film from the same laboratory shows Simons approaching an unsuspecting target individual on campus and asking him for directions. While the target is in full flow, a group of people carrying a door separate Simons from the target and stealthily replace Simons by Chabris. There is little physical similarity between the two. However the target carries on with his explanation unperturbed. When he is finished, Chabris asks the individual whether he had noticed anything odd. Yes, is the answer, he noticed being disturbed by people carrying a door. Then Simons makes his appearance and the target in some disarray suddenly realises what had gone on.

[1]   Simons, D.J. and Chabris. C.F. (1999), 'Gorillas in our midst: sustained inattentional blindness for dynamic events', *Perception*, **28** (9), 1059–1074.

Similar experiences involve the projection of still scenes, separated by a blank, in which vast areas of the scene are removed (New York skyline, the reflection of a building in a lake etc.) and this goes totally unnoticed by most of the audience. Strangely, if the separating blank is removed, the change becomes obvious. Then, without a blank, Kevin O'Regan of the Experimental Psychology Research Centre at the René Descartes University shows an image of a woman and a car in a busy street and asks whether, over a two minute period, anything has changed. Most viewers do not notice that the colour of the car has slowly changed from bright red to bright blue under their very eyes. The car occupies about 30% of the screen.

We will return to explanations of these phenomena, in the meantime it may be worth asking why are there shrieks of laughter, disarray and astonishment that accompany these phenomena. The reason may be this. Our sensory apparatus is normally highly reliable. If I wish to flick a grain of dandruff from my jacket, I feel that I know where it is with sufficient accuracy to apply the flick with delicacy and precision. So we feel that we have a mastery of our sensory world that allows us to act without error. When we fail to see the gorilla or a change in the person we are facing, this shakes our belief in our powers of perception and action to such an extent that we are embarrassed by it. We laugh in the way that we would had a magician caused a handkerchief to change colour under our very eyes or produced the proverbial rabbit out of the proverbial hat.

These effects go under the heading of 'inattention blindness' for the gorilla and 'change blindness' for the other two. In the rest of this chapter we examine the way in which people have reacted to these discoveries. Of course, the role of axioms and depictions will enter the discussion.

A grand illusion?

The severe shock that the above contingencies create has made commentators and scientists question whether we have a grasp on reality at all. The gorilla is clearly there, it may even hit our retina, but we have an impression of a reality that excludes it.

There is a salient publication that I wish to analyse here: *Is the Visual World a Grand Illusion?*[2] is a collection of views gathered by US philosopher Alva Noë '... to bring together the writings by philosophers and cognitive scientists that respond to a need for a better phenomenology of perceptual experience ...' (I will use the initials GI to refer to this collection).

But first, how does one define an illusion? With its usual authority, the Oxford dictionary uses the words: '... sensuous perception of an external object that involves a false belief. ...'. Or, in terms of a visual illusion: seeing something that is not there or not seeing something that is. There is also the class of well known visual illusions: lines that appear to be of different lengths when they are the same as measured by a ruler, or lines that appear to converge when they are parallel. These two examples are shown in Figure 5.1.

Are the two horizontal lines of equal length?   Are the two central lines parallel?

Figure 5.1 Well-known optical illusions.

This type of illusion is generally explained through an appeal to physiology: the receptive fields of the eye (neighbouring groups of retinal neurons that are processed together) are involved in making size judgements. When images cross the boundaries of such receptive fields they are judged differently from when they do not (left in fig 5.1). Similarly the movement of the fovea is diverted by the diagonal lines from judging the parallel lines (right in fig 5.1). Bruce Bridgeman of the University of Santa Cruz in California calls this a 'petit' illusion in GI, p. 29. Another type of well known illusions are 'ambiguous figures' as shown in fig. 5.2

---

[2]   Noë, A., ed. (2002), *Is the Visual World a Grand Illusion?* (Exeter: Imprint Academic).

Is it a duck or a rabbit?   Is X in front of Y?

Figure 5.2 Examples of ambiguous figures.

Here the fascination comes from the fact that we seem to see two things in each case, but not at the same time. These common illusions begin to introduce a tiny bit of doubt about the fact that things we see are always as they seem. However, the more dramatic effects of change and inattention blindness need more scrutiny if for no other reason than having evoked some strongly voiced opinions on how we delude ourselves that we perceive the world as it is. These are found in Noë's *Grand Illusion* (GI) collection an I examine some of them below.

Dennett's mistrust of inner worlds

It is generally acknowledged that (GI, p. 3) that the much-quoted Boston Philosopher, Daniel Dennett was one of the first to shatter our comfortable feeling that we are accurately aware of the sensory world we inhabit — the feeling that our experience is a smooth representation of some solid reality. He argued that our sensory apparatus is anything but a good translator of the real world, so, whatever it is that puts the sensory data together in our brains is telling lies by glossing over the gaps.[3] We end up having a mistaken sense of confidence that we know the way things are. He emphasizes two particular effects. The first is the fact that when our eye saccades from target to target it is blind during its trajectory, so whatever gets into our rosy sensation of the world has missed many things.

As Noë points out, this surely predicts the missing gorilla effect. While attending to the bouncing basketball, one's gaze

[3]   Dennett, D.C. (1992), *Consciousness Explained* (London: Allen Lane).

just does not alight on any part of the gorilla, leaving our experience bereft of it. Another piece of Dennett's evidence is the blind spot in our retinae. This is caused by a hole in the retinae that accommodate a bundle of optical nerve fibres which, strangely, originate on the inner part of the eyeball and need to convey retinal images to the brain. It is easy to show the existence of this blind spot through the use of fig. 5.3.

Figure 5.3 Close the right eye. Fixate on the star with the left and move your head away and towards the page at 20 to 30 centimetres. At some point, the smiley on the left will disappear.

How our awareness is deficient is actually easier to explain than our bewilderment when our errors are revealed. The 'how' has all to do with axioms 3 (attention) and 1 (depiction). We need to remind ourselves that the fovea, or accurate part of our retina only transmits accurately to the visual cortex a tiny part of our field of view. This is about the size of a character of print on this page held at a normal reading length. The rest, that is our sensation of a rich visual world out there, is likely to be due to the depictive mechanism of gaze-locked cells as discussed in Chapter 2 (axiom 1). But what is it that causes the fovea to move to certain points in the visual field? A whole lot of different events can. For example a change in illumination in time (flickering light) or space (moving object) is recorded by the cells in the less accurate surroundings of the retina, the perifovea. This signal is mapped onto the superior colliculus, a bit of brain whose output causes the eyes to move, causing the fovea to move to the disturbance in order to bring it into awareness. Events other than changes in the perifovea can influence the superior colliculus and make the eyes move. Examples are signals from higher brain centres as might be generated from an instruction to follow the basketball, or even sharp sounds. So it is clear that there could be a situation where the signals from the higher centres are in conflict with those coming from the perifovea and, lo and behold, the higher centres win and the gorilla is excluded from the depiction, that is, from the awareness.

The star/smiley case is only slightly different. The question here is why is it that we become aware of the blind spot only when following the rubric of fig. 5.3. Why is it that we are not aware of the hole in our vision all the time? First, there is the fact that both eyes are at work and the hole in each eye is in a different part of the total visual field. But if I look at the world with just one eye, because depiction takes place only from the content of the fovea, the hole is a part of the scene that is constantly missed. However, it is only under special conditions as created by the rubric in figure 5.3 do we become aware of the disappearance of perifoveal input. Notice that when fixating on the star with the left eye, there is never a total, rich sensation of the smiley, it's just some kind of black sign on white. Should this be something important that had disappeared from view as the head moved, the fovea would soon flick to the questionable area fleetingly to investigate what is happening, pick up and depict the missing part of the scene.

As already said above, neural effects which lead to seemingly fallacious experiences of the world are perhaps not as hard to explain as the astonishment experienced when these mistakes are pointed out. Dennett (GI, pp. 13–16) suggests that what is slighted is the theory we all form about the nature of our visual consciousness. We *feel* that we are perfect perceivers and this is like feeling that we are good lovers. Come a new relationship with a new partner and we may discover that we were just wrong about our own excellence. So we are wrong about a lot of things, and when errors are proved to us we react in explicit ways. But the fact is that we are not far from right in trusting our sense of a rich perception of the world probably as afforded by depictive mechanisms. It works well for us most of the time otherwise we would not be able to hit archery targets, shake hands with a friend, swat flies, scrump apples, recognise constellations and, indeed, flick dandruff off a sleeve. Missing gorillas and blind spots are special events that need a somewhat contrived scenario for their demonstration. So the surprise may partly be due to the fact that we recognise the nature of the contrivance and have feelings about it having fooled us. But I suspect that almost no-one who was impressed by the missing gorilla film will modify their attitude towards relying on their sense of visual awareness to such an extent as to begin to mistrust it.

Is the stream of consciousness an illusion?

As the argument develops that, after all, we can trust our confidence in our awareness of a real world, a number of eloquent commentators find it hard to relinquish the somewhat romantic idea that our grasp of the world is a bit of a dream, a bit of an illusion. In GI (p. 17), author Susan Blackmore argues that our smooth sensation of the world is, indeed an illusion. Her real target is the notion of there being 'a steam of consciousness', an idea attributed to William James at the end of the nineteenth century.[4] Introspection, he argues, provides a continuum during waking hours, it feels as if it flows like a stream. Blackmore argues vehemently that whatever our consciousness may be, it is not a continuous stream for the following reasons.

1. Much of vision is unconscious. How could things 'come into' consciousness?

2. If represented (or *depicted* in my terms) by neurons, how do we distinguish between neurons that contribute to consciousness and those that do not?

3. Change blindness is evidence against continuity.

4. In audition, picking out conversations from a hubbub or switching between different conversations is a sign of discontinuity.[5]

The real blockbuster question is the very first one and I shall return to it after looking briefly at the others. Question 2 has been answered by the hypothesis in Chapter 2 that suggests that a neuron has no chance of supporting a conscious sensation

[4]   James, W. (1890), *The Principles of Psychology* (London: MacMillan).
[5]   In passing, I note that Blackmore could have referred to the original framing of this problem by Colin Cherry in the 1950s as the 'cocktail party problem' and his subsequent studies on auditory attention.

unless it is locked to or referenced by muscular activity that is related to the positioning of events in the world (eye movement etc.). That is, in vision, only the depictive neurons, a minority among the total, are involved in consciousness. I shall deal with question 3 when discussing 'the sensorimotor contingency' later in this chapter. The fourth question is one of the very reasons that axiom 3, attention, is evoked in this book. Attention, both inner and outer is the sluice that diverts the stream (to go over-board on verbal metaphors). My name being called out by one speaker while I am listening to a conversation with another speaker about 'the traffic jam I got into in coming here', will interrupt that bit of excitement. My attention might switch to start listening to another stream about how 'it may be time to meet a new guest at the party'.

So, it remains necessary to return to the very important question of how things might actually come into stream-like consciousness from a discontinuous input. According to depictive/axiomatic ideas, what comes into consciousness is an overlap between perceptual and imaginational depictions. The former are reconstructions of input in space and time and the latter are triggered from a variety of sources including the perceptual depiction. Neural depictive processes however take a while to react, which means that they abhor instantaneous change. As neurons all have different delays they smooth out the imperfections and discontinuities of the early parts of the sensory process. I am talking of saccades and the like. To illustrate the point, figure 5.4 may be instructive.

It shows a depictive system consisting of only 16 cells. Some sensory input has half black and half white and the system has reached a stable depiction. The input then changes abruptly. The dynamic depictive system has to accommodate this change for it to come into consciousness. But we assume that, as in the brain, there are no synchronising clocks in the depictive mechanism. As in nature no two events can happen at the same time the state of only one cell can change at any one time. So, before the depictive network of cells can find a stable depiction, it is likely that some sequence of states as shown takes place in consciousness. The point is that depictive mechanisms have a dynamic of their own which smoothes imperfections and discontinuities of the visual apparatus. But because the world is a relatively non-jumpy place with its own abundance of inertia, the stream-lining effect of depictive apparatus, rather than giving us an illu-sory view of the world, is a way of not distorting the world due to the imperfections of our own apparatus.

In fact, the mechanism in fig. 5.4 explains a puzzle cited by Dennett in support of the illusion theory and echoed by Blackmore (GI, p. 25). This is the 'colour-phi' effect which takes place when a red light and a green light sited about 5 cm. from one another and at reading distance from the observer, flash alternatively, the red coming on when the green goes off and the green coming on when the red goes off. Some observers report that the light *moves* from one point to the other and changes col-our half way through. This is as if the right of the input in fig. 5.4 were red and the left green. The gradual transition would be sensed as a move with a change of colour when one colour begins to be depicted more than the other. Of course in the visual system of the brain, things are more complicated as change/ movement sensitive neurons as well as colour neurons are being stimulated, giving the same depiction as if the light had moved.

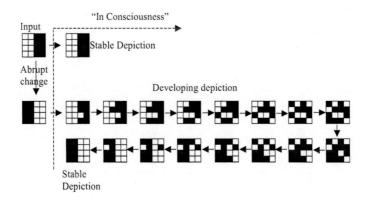

Figure 5.4 Changes in a dynamic depictive network due to an abrupt change in input.

So, personally, I cannot be as sceptical of a 'stream of consciousness' as is Susan Blackmore. William James was strug-
gling for words to describe what it is to be conscious. He chose
the word 'stream' to best encompass his feelings. I would argue
that 'a stream' is a good metaphor for the dynamic state changes
that may be occurring in depictive neural areas. In other words,
it is an irreversible, smooth sequence of state changes that occur
in axiom 1 and axiom 2 mechanisms when the sensory input
changes with time.

A new look at how we see: no illusion, just action?

It was psychologist Kevin O'Regan together with Californian
philosopher Alva Noë (O'R&N) who based a theory of vision on
the idea that change blindness and inattentional blindness
should not be 'explained away' as aberrations due to careless
attention in an otherwise rich and accurate perceptual system. In
2001 they published a seminal paper which drew both criticism
and support for proposing that 'the way we see' should undergo
a radical revision.[6] The thrust of this is to attempt to understand
better the role of attention which appears to be the thief that robs
our vision of gorillas and other major changes in the world. It
also suggests that there is no grand illusion, just a degree of automatic action that links input senses to motor actions. Specifically, they set out to address two puzzles:[7]

> How can we see at all if, in order to see we must first perceptu-
> ally attend to that which we see?

And

> If attention is required for perception, why does it seem to us as
> if we are perceptually aware of the whole detailed visual field
> when it is quite clear that we do not attend to the whole detail?

The first step in their argument is to distinguish between being
perceptually sensitive to sensory input and attending to it so as
to bring it into awareness. The example given is that we can

[6]   O'Regan, J.K. and Noë, A. (2001), 'A sensorimotor account of vision and
      visual consciousness', Behavioural and Brain Sciences, 24 (5).
[7]   Noë, A. and O'Regan, J.K. (2000), 'Perception, attention and the grand
      illusion', Psyche, 6 (15).

drive a car without attending to all the details of the road. But should a child suddenly jump into the road, we may well slam on the brakes before actually becoming conscious of what has happened. Noë and O'Regan call this kind of automatic link between perception and action *the rules of sensorimotor contingency*. These are rules that are built into living systems like the rules for homing in on a visual target might be in a guided missile. The organism is said to have *mastery* of the sensorimotor contingency rules if it can move itself or its sensory apparatus (e.g. eyes) to compensate for the peculiarities of the apparatus itself. For example, the superior colliculus that controls eye movement will cause the eyes to saccade exactly to the right spot in the world where a light might have just flicked on, despite the distortions and blind spots found on the retina.

Attention then, is the process of breaking into and controlling this sensorimotor activity. So one can be perceptually active without being aware, but one cannot be aware without being perceptually active. This solves the first puzzle: attention is a result of the sensorimotor contingency and perception is a kind of access of or 'breaking into' this process even though much of the detail of how 'breaking into' works, is missing.

The second puzzle is well illustrated in pictures such as fig. 5.5. In looking at the upper version of the picture, although we cannot see the detail, the rabbit appears as an entity. Noë and O'Regan argue that it is the sensorimotor contingency that gives us the feeling that 'if only I could get out there and remove the spots, I would see the whole rabbit'. And this, they argue, happens when we look around at anytime. Although our fovea is tiny we *know* that once having seen bits of the world we can get back to them at any time. So the world provides us with all the short-term memory we need to achieve this sensation of rich detail. It never needs to be reconstructed in the head: we are just masters of a lot of sensorimotor contingencies which leads us to appreciate the richness that is out there in the world.

Now, is it the case therefore, that having a rich world in our head despite the inaccuracy of our sensory equipment is a 'grand illusion'? Not so, say O'Regan and Noë. Most of us would not subscribe to the richness being in our heads (illusion) but

Figure 5.5 The upper rabbit figure feels almost as present as the lower despite being behind blobs.

realise that it's *only* out there (no illusion). The notion of a grand illusion is, therefore, wrong. In a sense it could be said that the world serves as the brain's short term memory. The sensation of richness comes from a sense of ability that if we want to access detail, it's out there for us to get it, no need to keep it in the head.

At this point the reader may wonder whether it is only the illusion theory which has been blown out of the water by sensorimotor contingency theory, or whether any idea of depiction and axioms has not been eliminated too. A comparison between the two approaches is necessary.

Axioms and sensorimotor contingencies

Sensorimotor contingency is discovered in several ways in the axiomatic, depictive descriptions of this book. The most obvious place is the mechanism of eye movement that involves the superior colliculus as mentioned earlier in this chapter. It is known that this, in a totally unconscious way, moves the fovea of the eye to places where things are happening (changes, movements, edges and so on …) which may be detected in the perifovea. But that is not all that causes the eye or, indeed, the head or body to move to bits of world that require attention: a sudden sound, the memory of having left the gas on in the kitchen, needing to check whether what is thought to be a familiar face, has correspondingly familiar features. Further, a strategy that involves memory and planning (axioms 2/4) can constrain foveal attention (e.g the basketball rather than the gorilla). Note that here I speak of 'external' attention mechanisms that correspond to sensorimotor contingencies. Whatever this mechanism might be, the results of attending are left in axiom 1 depictive machinery *for a while*. We recall that axiom 1 machinery is depictive by virtue of the fact that it 'knows' (i.e. encodes) the muscular effort that is being exerted in order to achieve a foveal position of the eyes. It is a mass of neurons that 'put things in place', but not for any length of time. It may be best to refer to fig. A7 in the appendix (p. 186 below). The perceptual module, I would argue, is active all the time and keeps a fading trace of experience which is accessible for a while, but does not necessarily lay down retrievable memories in the memory module.

I can then interpret the 'breaking in' through attention as a facilitation of the transfer of depictions from the perceptual module (axiom 1) to the memory module (axiom 2) where it will be a much paler version of what may briefly have been accurately depicted in the perceptual module, but where it will have a much more enduring and accessible existence. Then, according to axiom 3, the true function of attention is to control this facilitation. This requires a great deal more research and thought as to how such mechanisms work in the brain or even how they might work in a robot.

Axiomatic puzzle solving.

In the meantime one should be asking how do the axioms deal with the two puzzles outlined by O'Regan and Noë? They may be worth repeating. First:

> How can we see at all if, in order to see we must first perceptually attend to that which we see?

As stressed above, the key axiom here is 3 — attention. Attention is easily said but it is a complex concept and it may be found at many levels. First, as said above, the eye-moving superior colliculus can be influenced from a variety of sources some of which can be active ahead of depiction in axiom 1 and 2 mechanisms. It is quite true that in order to see, the basest mechanisms must be at work. As mentioned earlier, the effects of change, motion, edges are all automatic and pre-depictive. However, without them, according to axiom 1, depiction cannot happen. Second, deeper strategies for seeing are then triggered by the developing depiction. For example when a face is flashed suddenly on a previously blank screen, the foveal gaze will automatically be drawn to areas with much detail, such as an eye or the corner of a mouth. This will then be depicted causing the strategy of looking for base features to be switched to a higher level. Further saccades to where one might expect to find important features, such as the other eye or the mouth become controlled from axiom 2 mechanisms which are perceived even if the drive to find facial features may be somewhat automatic — like driving. There are even higher levels of search, for example, were a pair of twins distinguished by a little mole, having decided I am looking at one of the two, the search for the mole becomes a conscious affair driven strongly by the axiom 2 machinery.

Even ambiguous figures such as the duck/rabbit in fig.5.2 above, depend on hypothesis generation in axiom 2 mechanisms. Hypothesis, 'it's a duck' causes the eyes to choose switching the gaze between the eye of the image and its beak with the occasional saccade to the wiggle at the back of the head. Should the hypothesis be, 'it's a rabbit' the saccades become more frequent from eye to wiggle (seen as a mouth now) with the odd glance at the 'ears'. The reason this is an ambiguous illusion is that the low level attention triggers a hypothesis for a higher level interpretation (duck or rabbit) which then controls the higher level attention to execute a defined set of saccades. But a tiny perturbation can switch the whole system to settle into the alternative set of saccades.

So the answer to the first puzzle is that *perceptual* (i.e. conscious) attention is *not* necessary to begin to build up a depiction:
the process of base attention is innately automatic. Then as the
depiction is being built, and perception is developing, perceptual attention sets in, which allows the developing depiction in
axiom 1 mechanisms to allow hypotheses to emerge in axiom 2
memory mechanisms. I find it hard to describe this as a process
of 'breaking in', more a question of the sensorimotor contingency stimulating depictive knowledge.

The second puzzle is:

> If attention is required for perception, why does it seem to us as
> if we are perceptually aware of the whole detailed visual field
> when it is quite clear that we do not attend to the whole detail?

The second attentional mechanism mentioned above, where the
depictive mechanism (ax. 2 machinery) drives attention to fill
important gaps in depiction, clearly stops at some point where
sufficient detail is present in the depiction. This is pretty rich and
satisfying even if all the available detail may not be included. In
fact this theory explains why we are not so bothered by the black
blobs over the rabbit and why the 'presence' of the rabbit (fig.
5.5) is similar for the upper and lower images. The detail in each
of the images causes very similar attention strategies to be
unleashed, and these are due to the rabbit rather than the blobs.
As indicated by the axiomatic/depictive theory it's the interplay
between the mechanisms of the fist three axioms that give us the
sense of a rich world. It may not be complete, but what is there is
sufficient for our needs and therefore satisfying even if not all
gorillas are accounted for or, helpfully, if blobs don't get in the
way of what really draws our attention.

The illusion partisans

Even though the case for visual consciousness as an illusion is
looking a little shaky, there are several adherents to it in GI. Eric
Schwitzgebel of the philosophy department at the University of
California at Riverside chooses mental imagery as his target (GI,
p. 35) arguing that we delude ourselves about how good this
imagery actually is. The 'illusion' in his thesis is not that we

remember things that we had never seen (although this can happen), but that we make mistaken judgements about the *quality* of our visual memory. Through a series of tests he shows that the participants in his experiments, while initially confident in their capacity for visual imagery, find it really hard to answer his questions about their imaginational visual experience. This shakes their confidence. This is also at odds with received wisdom from psychological experiments of the kind that measure people's ability to 'rotate' images in their heads and the vividness of their experience. The axioms have little to say about this except that the first three mechanisms are needed to ensure that we have visual memory at all. Of course we rely on this for our own cognitive success (say, visualising how to get from home to work) and helping others (telling them how get to my place for a dinner party). Some things such as the rapid sequence of events of an accident may be hard to visualise as axiom 2 machinery may not have had sufficient time to form accessible attractors. We may also be surprised by an external measurement of our imaginational prowess which may be less than we had thought. But this is no different from discovering that having thought that I was 1m 80cm in height, I discover that it's really 1m 75cm. Our estimation errors should not be confused with illusions. Under normal conditions, our visual memory serves us sufficiently well most of the time and that's all we need to know.

However, scepticism of simple models of visual consciousness dies hard. Temre Davies, Donald Hoffman and Antonio Rodriguez of the University of California at Irvine have mounted an interesting attack on what they call the 'standard account' of vision (GI, p. 72). By 'standard account' they refer to a theory of vision that goes back to the pioneering work of David Marr, an Englishman who emigrated in the late 1970s to the Massachusetts Institute of Technology.[8] According to this account, the brain receives fragments of the scene: glints, textures, edges, shadings and so no. It then *reconstructs* from them, stage by stage, a palpable and accurate representation of the objects that

[8]   Marr, D. (1982), *Vision: A Computational Investigation into the Human Representation and Processing of Visual Information* (San Francisco: Freeman).

are out there in the world. The point stressed by these authors is not that such detailed reconstructions are impossible, but that they are unnecessary. What they call 'constructions' will do. That is, the detailed fragments must be represented in some way as fleeting signatures in the brain. This is sufficient for the organism to survive successfully in its environment. The 'illusion' element of this work is the mistaken belief that a reconstruction of objects localised in the brain needs take place.

Does this criticism apply to the depictive theories expressed in this book? I would say not and add that it accords with them. A depiction is not a reconstruction of objects. It is what the Irvine authors call a construction, but with the added twist that the construction is indexed (as stressed in Chapter 2) according to where tiny foveal fragments are in the world. I agree that 'objects' need not be carefully reconstructed for visual sensation to be rich and satisfying. Objects are more to do with foveal exploration, planning and action triggered by the content of constructions, or the state of axiom 2 machinery in our terms.

The Tinkerbell effect

Tinkerbell is that self-sacrificing fairy in Peter Pan, who, when dying from having taken the poison aimed at Peter Pan, can be saved were the audience to *will* this to happen. Frank Durgin, a psychologist at Swarthmore College in the US used the good fairy's name to describe a strange visual effect (GI, p. 88). Flashes of light disposed in a circle are displayed on a screen through a program that finds positions for the flashes totally at random. Audiences observing this are asked whether they can *will* a clockwise or counter clockwise motion to be discerned in what they see. The answer is that they can, that the speed of this apparent motion can measured and that different participants see the motion in opposite directions from the same stimulus.

Durgin sees this result as supporting the Grand Illusion by arguing (as has been done by others for some years) that the visual system of the brain is an imaginational activity superimposed on sensory data. In other words, this is not very different from what we see when we look at the cube in figure 5.2. We can will the cube to be one way as opposed to another. But this is clearly the work of the brain and not the environment. However, it is not enough to say that this is an imaginational activity super-imposed on sensory data. The key mechanism or the missing link in understanding this phenomenon is visual attention, that is, eye movement. As in the case of ambiguous figures it is the movement of the eyes that is driven by a hypothesis of what may be the content of axiom 2 machinery. The *willing* in the Tinkerbell experiments may well be accompanied by anticipa-tory eye movements which then *attend* to those random flashes that are consistent with the desired direction of the motion. This creates an expectation in axiom 3 machinery which controls attention, which strengthens the expectation and so on ...

So, yet again, this is not so much a Grand Illusion as the fact that taking the mechanisms of perception, imagination and attention together, we find a highly pro-active system that is continually attempting to extract information from the world that makes the organism ready to engage with this world.

Back in the philosophers' cave

Most of the arguments so far, as to whether our sense of vision is an illusion or not, have a psychological basis and are carried out amongst those who have psychological interests. That is, they ask whether there are elements of this illusion which are likely to affect behaviour or the inner cognitive states of living organ-isms? But philosophers too have an interest although from a dif-ferent slant: how logical are the arguments about illusions? Some philosophers have expressed their thoughts in the GI col-lection. For example Jonathan Cohen, a philosopher from the University of California at San Diego, writes of the 'Grand Grand Illusion Illusion' meaning that he feels that grand illusion arguments are flawed (GI, p. 141).

Yes, Change Blindness and Inattention Blindness are effects that surprise the average person and should therefore be fully investigated as psychological phenomena. But they do not reveal an illusional aspect of consciousness, that is, conscious-ness providing false experiences of a real world. This, they argue, is so for three main reasons. First, the belief in a rich sensation of the world is not actually denied by the unusual examples of blindness. It merely seems odd that such things can happen *given* that we have a rich sensation which most of the time is true enough to serve us well. Second, the idea that it destroys our illusion of having 'snapshots in the head' is false to the extent that only computer scientists or neuroscientists may have advanced such models. The average observer of the visual world will not naturally believe this. At least, seeing seems a natural activity which does not necessarily feel as if it is some photographic process in the head.

I once gave a talk to very young people about how one can make computers that 'see'. At the end of the lecture a girl aged about nine stood up and said, 'Your computers must be really stupid. Seeing is easy, even my little brother can see. But if you could give me a computer to do my sums for me, that's something I would really like.' Clearly this took place before the advent of the home computer. But it makes the point that seeing seems so natural that people don't theorise about it. Cohen's third point is similar: illusion theory questions the existence of inner representations which are used by the conscious organism to develop its actions. If Fred tries to remember how to get from his home to the grocery shop, it's not helpful for someone to say to him that the visual memory he has of how to get there is an illusion. He will not take kindly to the idea that his thoughts that lead him to the shop are some kind of unreliable dream. He just happily wonders off to the grocery shop. Again it is only the scientist who is left arguing about how this can happen.

On the other hand, Mark Rowlands Professor of Mental and Moral Philosophy at the University of Hertfordshire, sees the blindness work of Noë and O'Regan as supporting his own view that having a conscious experience occurs in virtue of the fact that there is an active intention by the organism to apply its sensory apparatus to something. The something is 'out there' and not in the head. What about mental imagery? OK, he says, so some phenomenal experience is internally constituted, but this does not mean that all consciousness is so constituted. This is precisely why in my own axioms there is an appeal to three distinct axioms which then allows us to appreciate the difference between the perception of the out-there world (in axiom 1 machinery) and internal memories of it (axiom 2) and that attention (axiom 3) mediates between the two. But Rowlands' claim (and, indeed that of Noë and O'Regan) that in having an experience there is *no* inner representation seems too dramatic. The trouble with inhabitants of the philosophers' cave is that they appear to generate monolithic theories about things. There either is or there is not internal representation. The fact is that the brain wins every time. It will have evolved some aspects of consciousness that do rely on something like sensorimotor contingencies and other aspects that rely heavily on depictions both of current sensory input and of memory. They work together in ways that are perhaps less mysterious for engineers than philosophers. It's a bit like trying to have a philosophy relating to why an aeroplane flies. One theory could be based on wing shape, and another on engine thrust. Of course, the engineer knows that both are necessary to have a complete explanation.

An area that Rowlands finds unpalatable however, is that by eliminating inner representation, O'Regan and Noë have eliminated the 'explanatory gap' between representation and sensation (see Chapter 7). Interestingly, here, Rowlands does refer to consciousness of imagined things to say that the problem has not gone away. Of course, axiomatic theory simply (controversially, perhaps) equates the existence of depictions with the existence of sensory experience eliminating the gap that way. But, I have no doubt that this does not go down well in the philosophers' cave.

A philosophical last word: the ping pong robot

Still among philosophers, the last word in GI goes to Andy Clark, a British philosopher at Indiana University in the US at the time of making his contribution (p. 181). Like Mark Rowlands he extracts the central claim that O'Regan and Noë have made in their 2001 paper that there are no inner representations. So what are experiences? According to the controversial authors they are not inner states, but are ways of acting, they are things we do. Clark suggests thinking of a simple ping-pong playing robot with a paddle held by an arm and a hand, a good vision system based on stereo cameras. It has circuitry that predicts the trajectory of the ping pong ball and calculates where the paddle should be to return the ball. There is a system within the robot that measures performance and is capable of tuning the paddle-driving mechanism so that the amount of calculation is reduced and the response becomes automatic when the ball is seen in flight. This is the kind of thing that artificial neural networks can do quite well. Another program can then adjust the performance of the system to set its prowess to the skills of an opponent, so as to provide a challenging game.

This system has mastery of a sensorimotor activity and a link to 'thought' or planning programs. That is, it has all the requirements that satisfy O'Regan and Noë's conditions for the presence of consciousness. But, as Clark points out, the attribution of qualitative consciousness is out of place here. Noë and O'Regan have replied to this line of argument by saying that it is a matter of scale: the thought processes of the robot are not sufficiently developed to be considered as taking part in the process of being conscious. Of course this puts back into question 'what it is to be conscious?'. If being conscious is not contained in *all* mechanisms that comply with 'sensorimotor contingency' theory, then the theory is incomplete.

This is why, in the axiomatic/depictive ideas of this book I have insisted that all five axioms need to be satisfied for an organism to be considered to be conscious. As Clark's robot example stresses, and the sensorimotor contingency authors agree, something is missing. While 'sensorimotor' ideas encompass axiom 3 attention and axiom 1 engagement with the world, there is no axiom 2 machinery which is necessary to provide 'thought processes that are sufficiently complex' for the robot to be considered as being conscious.

Rounding off: the gorilla is forgiven
To some readers, the idea of a Grand Illusion of the visual world must come across as a somewhat dubious notion. Initiated by

experiments that clearly show that we are not aware of all that happens before our eyes, it turns out that there are mechanistic and philosophical arguments that show this not to be an illusion in the sense that we see things that are false or ambiguous. It is more a function of the restrictions on ways that our sensory systems can work: eyes dart about to allow the brain to make as much sense of the world as possible, but this does miss the odd gorilla. The more significant result of these strange results of being blind of some things is that it has given birth to the 'sensorimotor contingency' theory of O'Regan and Noë which questions, and, according to some, eliminates the idea that seeing is a process of representations in the brain. I have argued against this by suggesting that depicting the world through neural action in the brain is a rather special form of representation which not only explains how attention becomes a very important process in giving us a feeling of the world 'out there' but how it is a key part of creating visual memory. Sensorimotor contingency theory is clearly a most important way of looking at becoming conscious particularly of visual things. However, the view that this chapter has provided while appreciating the importance of this way of thinking, indicates that it is still too early to believe that Noë and O'Regan have provided a complete model of what it is to be conscious. Who knows? Perhaps in combination with axiomatic, depictive ideas, progress towards a unified theory can be made.

Chapter 6

Knowing What We Want

Is free will an illusion?

Why is it that 'free will' is a deep and ancient philosophical and theological problem? I know that within the limits of decency and the law, I can be clear about my desires and attempt to follow them. Do I choose to be a lawyer or a baker, put on a classical or a jazz record, lead a dedicated or a profligate life, eat pizza or pasta at the restaurant? We make our decisions according to what feels like a reasoned way and take actions to achieve what we want. This would normally be called a 'folk' view of taking decisions, and for most purposes of getting on with life, no more needs be said. But then a niggling question begins to disturb this peaceful conclusion: what in our brains determines whether I choose pizza or pasta given that I like both and the decision almost feels arbitrary? How free is my desire, my volition? What are the factors that determine which choice I will make? Is what I shall actually do predetermined in some way? How true is the involvement of axioms 4 (planning using knowledge and imagination) and 5 (emotion as an evaluator of my plans) in the exercise of volition?

As with many other 'folk' theories of mental life, what we naturally think about free will is a product of the culture in which we live. And, a little circularly, culture is what people think and do, and pass on to us when we are young. This is always fashioned by what has been recorded of the wise thoughts of our ancestors. So, in this chapter, I shall first try to see how 'free will' has been thought of through the ages. This, in order to colour in the background to the fact that 'free will' is an integral part of our consciousness and is therefore a matter for brain science and, through the axioms, a matter for which one might try to identify mechanisms that can be said to possess it.

Talking of brain science, it was in the context of neuroscience that Californian physiologist Benjamin Libet who, in the 1980s, *measured* the brain response to 'wanting something'. He made an astonishing discovery. The brain activity is not a response at all but an *anticipation* by nearly one second of becoming conscious of wanting. This hit the world of neuroscience by storm casting doubt on almost any form of folk neuro-theory where wanting would have to be directly accompanied by brain activity. It is this discovery that led Harvard psychologist Dan Wegner to argue that determining what we want is not based on conscious brain activity at all, but some unconscious occurrence which both determines what we want and how we go and get it. Wegner argues that what we feel about having caused things in the world to happen by willing it is false. Conscious will is an illusion![1]

In the second half of this chapter, I will show that the axioms provide a more optimistic outlook. Yes, we may not be entirely conscious of how intention links to action, but the link could be a mechanistically true one rather than a mysterious illusion. But first, what is our cultural heritage when it comes to will and its freedom?

Ancient Greece

One would normally expect that the Greek 'greats', Socrates, Plato and Aristotole would have laid the foundation for discussing the nature of free will. But they did so only indirectly, by attempting to explain what is the nature of the thinking part of a human being. It was only later in philosophy that it was recognised that volition was a powerful part of thought which required deeper attention. Aristotle (384 –382 b.c.) conceived the

---

[1]   Wegner. D.M. (2002), *The Illusion of Conscious Will* (Cambridge MA: MIT Press).

thinking part of a living organism as its 'form'. For Aristotle, 'form' was the essence of an object. The 'matter' of a spoon may be wood, but the form of a spoon is its 'spoonness' which includes a knowledge of what the spoon does. So a living organism, a human, has a special form. What it does is to think. This is a 'soul' which for Aristotle was very much a living property that perished with the death of the body. This contrasts with the earlier thoughts of Socrates (470–399 BC) as interpreted by Plato (427–348 BC) in which the thinking soul survives the death of the body. This emerges from a somewhat unclear argument about life coming from death and death coming from life. The soul survives in Hades awaiting the coming to life again.

Aristotle avoided this mystique by specifically allowing that 'soul' is the very property of a body that distinguishes between a live being and a corpse. Implicit in this, is a form of will linked to a soul which even in animals, is responsible for movement as well as a perception of the world. What moves must have the will to move. Humans have the additional feature of 'imagination' in their souls, which can also determine movement. In this way Aristotle anticipated the notion of a mind or even consciousness which were to surface later in the history of philosophy. So the ticking philosophical time bomb of free will lies hidden in the Aristotelian soul. If the soul manages movement, something linked to perception and imagination must be causing the action.

The British philosopher, D.W. Hamlyn in his *History of Western Philosophy*[2] suggests that the freedom of will was implicit in the beliefs of Greece. However it only surfaced among the Stoics of 300 b.c. who inherited an older belief of a rigorous atomism: all was made of atoms that interacted through very strict determined rules to fashion the objects of the world. But if this were true, any thought of a 'free' will might have to be abandoned because the behaviour of the atoms is predetermined. This later became the classical dilemma of free will — if science can predict

[2]   Hamlyn, D.W. (1990), *The Penguin History of Western Philosophy* (London: Penguin Books). I shall make frequent references to Hamlyn's excellent source book as [DWH].

things and will can be scientifically studied, then it is not free, or freedom does not have a scientific meaning.

It was Epicurus (341–270 BC) — the very same philosopher who advocated the enjoyment of life and eating — who suggested that atoms, in their passage through the soul can perform unexpected 'swerves' leaving open a certain arbitrariness of choice in determining actions. Could 'free' be interpreted as 'arbitrary'? This question persists to the present day.

More generally, the Stoics believed that we choose actions in function of our specific natures which differ from individual to individual. This 'soft determinism' crops up now and then in more modern philosophies always leaving open the question of whether individuals with individual action destinies are still constrained by some major universal cause.

So, by the beginning of the quarter century BC, will had not explicitly received the attention of the great philosophers. And yet it formed a niggling question at the back of thinkers' minds: how does thought link to action and how independent is such thought?

The next 1600 years

Did philosophy grind to a halt after the impact of the greats in 300 BC? Historians sometime argue that after Aristotle, the inventive quality of philosophy in Greece had declined. But historians also recognise the value of post-Aristotelian thinking of the so-called Neo-Platonists (for example, Plotinus, 204 –269 AD and Porphyry, 233–304 AD) who did worry about will, recognising that the abstract soul linked thought and matter through influencing movement. But the focus of philosophy during this period was shifting towards Christian Europe particularly with the powerful contribution of Augustine (354–430 AD). As a Christian philosopher he held the soul in a position of central importance in controlling perception and imagination.

Interestingly, for Augustine, what is perceived involves an act of will, which gives individuals individual ways of developing their souls. Will features as a strong element in Augustine's beliefs as the means by which an individual attains happiness in the quest to please God and identify with him. 'Freedom' is found in the ability to *not* follow the favoured path, thus resulting in a sort of passive evil. Therefore, putting this with much less sophistication than found in Augustine, the soul of a human being is free to develop its own character of being good or evil, a character which can be submitted to divine judgement. But the problem of what drives the soul into its choices remains, and the question of what constitutes freedom is further established with Augustine as a philosophical challenge for his followers.

This concern is evident in the philosophy of the next 900 years. For example, Boethius (480–524) reasoned that God, from his point of view of eternal timelessness sees the decisions of humans as having been freely made. His knowledge of them does not change the fact that, because time exists for humans, they will have experienced decision points at which their choices appeared free.

It was not only Christian philosophy that attempted to grapple with issues of the omniscience of God and the freedom of the human will. In the Arab world of Moorish Spain, Aristotle was being rediscovered and appreciated. For example, Averroes (Arab name, Ibn Rushd: 1126–1198) re-stated the Aristotelian notion that intellect, as the main component of the soul, perishes with the death of the body. This would have been blasphemy in Christianity. Averroes also concurred with the view of God as the ultimate element of pure form in a continuum from form to matter. This gave God a supreme abstract position that would not need to be concerned with interactions with matter and would therefore not need the power of will. This is only a necessity for the human intellect.

It was this revival of Aristotelian ideas that influenced the philosophy of Christian theologian Thomas Aquinas (1225–1274). A Dominican who taught in Paris and Italy and who, despite the need to deny the mortality of the soul as expounded by Averroes, embraced the view of God as pure form. His thoughts on will were also Aristotelian: it is the pursuit of happiness that moves the intellect towards pure form, that is, towards unity with God. Will is that element of thought that encourages such positive thought, while failure in this endeavour results in a passive evil akin to that of Augustine. Whether will is entirely free remains unclear despite the observation that both good and evil individuals exist.

It is not within the scope of this discourse to look closely at the contributions to philosophy by the important figures of John Duns Scotus (1266–1308) and William of Ockham (1285–1349). They both saw will as towering over intellect and being totally unconstrained but dependent on a moral sense for leading to 'good' actions. While the details of this might be left to the reader, I think that I have stressed sufficiently that even in mediaeval times the wilful achievement of desires and the quality of such desires was a difficult matter for explanation. There was no science to speak of, and religious doctrines placed strong constraints on what could be believed. This then was the background to the epochs that followed: the renaissance and the scientific age of rationalism.

The renaissance and rationalism

It is generally acknowledged that during the Renaissance in the Europe of the fifteenth and sixteenth centuries, some of the finest works of art, literature and architecture were bequeathed to the world to be admired in perpetuity. But not so in philosophy, argues D.W. Hamlyn. The grip of dogma was being lessened and this left a kind of philosophical vacuum that would take some time to fill. Nevertheless examples of innovative thought may be found. Notable is the work of Francis Bacon (1561–1626) and Thomas Hobbes (1588–1626) who were concerned with finding sound frameworks for philosophical enquiry. The latter, despite being best appreciated for his political philosophy, expressed a view on perception and the will. He wrote of 'motions' within the body which, when caused externally were responsible for perception. When such motions were initiated internally they could lead to acts of volition. Desires are explained as originating in internal motions and leading to external action. When desires are achieved we are pleased, and otherwise we may be displeased. This is an early suggestion that there may be a link between will and emotion, a mechanism that features in the axiomatic view that is expressed at the end of this chapter. In fact, if for 'motions' we read 'neural activity' it is interesting to see how close Hobbes' explanation of will comes to the mechanistic neural explanation (axioms 4 and 5) that we shall see later.

The word 'rationalism' is generally reserved for Descartes and his followers. Descartes (1596–1650) is the giant who set philosophy on an entirely new path. Most are familiar with his pronouncement *cogito ergo sum* (I think therefore I am). But why is this seemingly simple statement the headline of a philosophical revolution? To me, the answer seems to be this. Since Aristotle, the human being was seen as a material body that *has* a thinking component, the soul. With Descartes, the being itself *is* a thinking thing that becomes aware of its own existence through the ability to think. This conclusion is reached through knowing that thought can be false through being based in mistaken beliefs. But there is one thought that cannot be: the thought that one exists. Therefore being a thinking thing is a universally true thought. A 'first' in the history of philosophy.

Yes, Descartes recognised the existence of the material body, but it is its thinking nature, its 'mind' that makes the individual conscious of his own existence that represents a departure from older philosophy and the influence of Aristotle. Primarily, mind becomes distinguished from the Aristotelian soul. It is mortal, and, Descartes believed, it is linked to the material body (brain) through the pineal gland. The soul becomes a matter of theological belief rather than rational philosophy. Also 'dualism' is born: the philosophy that detaches mind and consciousness from brain. As we shall see in chapter 7, this has its influence even today in Chalmers' formulation of the 'hard problem'. Will, in the Cartesian system, is a property of mind as are perception and imagination. All these are gifts of God and will is free as God has created rational beings, beings who can choose among available actions and use reason to distinguish truths from falsehoods.

The concept of the rational individual was a powerful thought that other thinkers were quick to accept. Benedict de Spinoza (1632–1677), the reclusive Dutch lens grinder, subjected the idea to a rigorous and systematic analysis. For him, given the realisation of existence, will is the endeavour of an organism 'to persist in its own being'. Spinoza identifies emotions as elements that are adverse to the purposes of the organism in its endeavour to persist in its existence. Will is that part of rational thought that prevents thought from being trapped by the emotions. Clearly, my view that gives rise to the emotion axiom (5) does not concur with Spinoza in this respect. For me emotions evaluate planning so as to allow the organism to *achieve* its desires — they are not constraints.

An extravert in comparison with Spinoza, German philosopher Gottfried Leibniz (1646–1716), saw the rational individual as embedded in 'the best of all possible worlds' as created by God. He argued that everything that people do has reasons in this world, but the reasons 'incline' rather than 'necessitate' [DWH]. Will is again the element of thought that assesses these inclinations, ultimately leading to actions. This accords entirely with the axiomatic theory.

British empiricism

Empiricism is an observational science, and it is John Locke (1632–1704), a native of Wrington in Somerset, who is seen to have established the school of British empirical philosophy. The empirical character of Locke's philosophy comes from his reluctance to follow Descartes in abstract speculation of how mind links to body, preferring to look closely at the distinguishing features of that which mind contains: knowledge, ideas and opinions. Incidentally, Locke was also innocently responsible for bringing the word *consciousness* into prominence as the material for his philosophy was drawn from 'that of which I am conscious'. Will for Locke comes from being conscious of power. We know what we can do and use this to direct our 'operative faculties to motion or to rest' (quoted in [DWH]). Axiomatically, 'to know what we can do' is to exercise axiom 4 planning in axiom 2 machinery. How this might relate to 'operative faculties' will be explained towards the end of this chapter.

Locke's concern with the importance of ideas had a profound effect on the theologian George Berkeley (1685–1753) who took the point to an extreme. He argued that whatever object that we are able to consider *only* exists as an idea in our minds. This is an ultimate form of 'idealism' which met with some ridicule at the time. But Berkeley used it as an argument for the role of God who ensures the continuation of a real world as it is a sustained idea in His mind. Idealism survived longer than one might think and was only robustly denied in the twentieth century (by George Moore among others), as we shall see. In axiomatic terms, there is no scope for extreme idealism, as axiom 1 assumes the existence of a world independent of those who observe it.

But the empiricist who turned out to be most influential in shaping current discussions about will was the Scottish sceptic, David Hume (1711–1776). Causality was one of his targets. We cannot reason about causality because our experience only gives us a conjunction of events. Reasoning that clouds cause rain is merely reasoning that we observe that one event often follows another. While we can experience the clouds and we can experience the rain, we cannot experience the causation. This is a rather extreme view that denies much scientific method, but it is quoted by those who argue that free will is an illusion in the sense that we cannot *sense* causation even if it is the causation of our thoughts on our actions. More of this later.

German philosophy into the nineteenth century.

Immanuel Kant (1724–1804) is spoken of in reverent tones as one of the most influential philosophers after Descartes. He distinguished those ideas that we acquire by observation and definition (e.g. birds have wings) from those that we possess or absorb 'naturally' (a ball rolls down a slope). He endowed the mind with strong organisational powers which defined the objects of the world. His was a latter day form of idealism. He had a special category for 'free will' alongside the existence of God and the immortality of the soul. He saw it as a necessary belief rather than a fundamental property of thought. The belief would entail the morals of action and a consciousness of departures from such morals.

Georg Hegel (1770–1831) continued German philosophy in the idealist style giving much prominence to the world within. It was the spiritual nature of reality that was important to him rather than the definition of objects as ideas that was advocated by Kant. This spiritual notion of the world evolved towards an 'absolute' sense of knowledge by considering propositions and their opposites. From this a rigorous conclusion could be drawn, which might become a proposition for the next round of evolution of thought. He sees free will in the backdrop of human institutions: the state, the community, the family. Obedience to communal 'will' is the 'good' way of using will, contributing to the integrity of the communal benefit.

Finally, Arthur Schopenhauer (1788–1860) disagreed with the spirituality of Hegel while seeing some good in the objects-as-ideas idealism of Kant. Prolific on the question of will, he was also depressingly pessimistic in his outlook. Will as a continuous force to satisfy one's desires leads to disappointment as desires can never be totally fulfilled. Will is the source of human suffering. For example desires such as for love from a sexual partner might remain unfulfilled due to the impulsive and inappropriate nature of the will to satisfy sexual desire. This pessimistic perspective has left its mark in both literature and later philosophy, for example, that of Friedrich Nietzsche (1844–1900). It is quite true that when we feel depressed, the thought of wanting to do things feels negative and adds to the depression. For me, the interpretation of will as a depressive notion is very much associated with Schopenhauer and seems not to have influenced philosophical thought in a fundamental way.

The twentieth century

The twentieth century was a time of excitement in philosophy not only because of the positivism and linguistic philosophy of Russell, Wittgenstein and Ayer, but also because of the proliferation in higher education which meant that more students could access new philosophical ideas. Positivism is the intention to base philosophy on empirical knowledge of physical phenomena. Linguistic philosophy concerns itself with the clarification of language. I shall not review these trends in any detail as they concerned more with natural phenomena as perceived through sensory experience and the way we then talk about them. While these are enormously important as they have influenced the axiomatic method, there is not much emphasis on will and emotion. However, I wish briefly to mention two twentieth-century philosophers who did have a significant impact on the problem of free will. They are Moore and Sartre.

George Edward Moore, (1873–1958), British philosopher who taught at Cambridge University between the wars, led a robust reinstatement of realism in philosophy. While not at all at odds with the positivist and linguistic ideas of focusing on sensory experience, his view of will had the pragmatic character of noting that we appreciate the world as it is and, within this, we are able to develop apt choices of how to act. The axiomatic view accords with this as it is the basis of the planning axiom, 4.

If anyone was concerned with 'freedom' to the point of obsession, it was Jean-Paul Sartre. Left-wing hero of twentieth-century philosophy, he established 'existentialism' as a world movement. Largely conceived by the nineteenth-century Danish philosopher Søren Kierkegaard, existentialism is a philosophy of personal freedom unconstrained by dicta or dogma. Personal passion features strongly in making choices: recognising personal responsibility is the guiding principle in making choices. Sartre wrote of the failure of individuals to recognise their freedom and the need to exercise it with responsibility when they attribute their actions to institutions and customs. Interestingly he reconciled this with Marxism by arguing that real responsibility is best exercised in collective movements that develop a collective sense of will.

The cultural 'folk theory'.

The point of taking the above journey through philosophical theory is to show that whatever 'folk' theory of will we possess, this is not arbitrary but is both shaped by and indicative of concerns that date back 2500 years. In feeling that we can make arbitrary decisions we are at one with Epicurus and his random 'swerves'. Our *need* to feel free in our decisions was recognised by the Stoics. While should we feel that our will is in some way that of God, we rely on Augustine and Aquinas for reassurance that God created us with an intellect akin to his own which embodies a free will. Descartes influences us by arguing that without divinely endowed freedom to recognise both truth and falsehood we would be automata unworthy of divine creation.

The British Empiricists and the German formalists are in the background when we feel that the freedom of will is not 'just another thought' but something rather special. Moore and Sartre are at work when we note that our will relates to the real world and this implies a responsibility towards others. This does not mean that individuals would be ignorant of their sense of will had they not read this philosophy. On the contrary, it means that philosophers concern themselves with things that we and they, as humans, would like to elaborate and add to the corpus of both formal and 'folk' philosophy

So it is easy to see that philosophers and other individuals alike will suffer a sense of shock were they told that folk feelings of will are nought but an illusion!

Libet's bombshell.

It is part of the every-day work of physiologists to attempt to measure the correlation between events that occur in the brain and their accompanying inner sensation. Benjamin Libet at the University of California at Santa Fé, was interested in acts of will and their brain correlates. In particular, in 1983[3] he and his colleagues wanted to measure the time it took between wanting to do something and doing it. He devised an experiment where the decision to do something had an arbitrariness about it. In line with other similar experiments, he measured the electro-encephalographic recording (EEG) that related to wanting to lift a finger at a time arbitrarily selected by the participant, and the moment of lifting the finger.

---

[3]   Libet, B., Wright, E.W. and Pearl, D. K. (1983), 'Time of conscious intention to act in relation to onset of cerebral activity (readiness potential): The unconscious initiation of a free voluntary act', *Brain* , **106**, 623–642.

Normally this experiment would measure the time of the brain activity when wanting to lift the finger (Bw) and then, the time of both the brain activity that lifts the finger (Bl) and the actual moment of lifting the finger (L). It was thought that Bl would occur a small fraction of a second after Bw followed another fraction of a second later by by L. All of this accords with the folk idea that we need brain activity to want something and that a little later this causes other brain activity that activates the muscles that unleash the desired physical action.

To add greater interest to the experiment Libet invented an ingenious way of measuring the moment at which the conscious thought of lifting the finger occurred to the participant. He asked the participant to observe a dot moving in a circular trajectory on the screen, the trajectory being marked with numbers and to note the number when the conscious thought of lifting the finger occurred. This acted like a clock. Of course the experimenter expected this reading to coincide with the brain activity Bw. The surprise came when it transpired that (Bw) occurred half to three-quarters of a second *before* the participant became conscious of 'wanting'. This brain activity then became known as the 'Readiness Potential' which somehow unconsciously anticipated consciousness a volitional event.

An obvious interpretation of this result is that the conscious will to do something is not the free event we feel, but it is dependent on an unconscious occurrence in the brain that is initiated in a way that is as yet not properly understood. This theme is taken up in an argument that free will is an illusion.

Wegner's illusory sense of will

Dan Wegner, a professor of Psychology at Harvard University was quick to recognise the philosophical significance of Libet's finding. He encompassed the situation by proclaiming the 'theory of apparent mental causation':

> People experience conscious will when they interpret their own thought as the cause of their action.

So a totally unconscious neural event causes the wanting and it causes the action a little later. This feels as if the action is caused by the wanting, but the link is said to be entirely illusory. It's a bit like 'willing' the traffic lights to change, which they always do, but there is no link, no causation just one event following another.

Wegner presents several other examples of involuntary actions in his book[1]. Hypnosis and various forms of automatic acts sometimes due to brain lesions are brought to the fore by Wegner to demonstrate that will and action are not necessarily intimately related.

At this point I need to express a little scepticism on the rush to interpret Libet's results as defining free will as an illusion. First one needs to question exactly what it is that is measured and labelled as Bw. Second, I shall show that the illusion model is just one interpretation of Libet's result: there are others that do not involve illusions. For this we appeal to some simple axiomatic neuromodelling.

An axiomatic neuromodel

I reproduce here with a few more appropriate labels, the 'kernel' machinery that supports the five axioms and which has been discussed in the Appendix (fig A7).

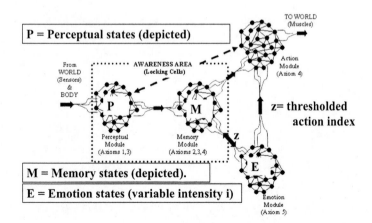

Fig. 6.1 Labelled version of the architecture that supports the axioms (Appendix)

To illustrate the way that this architecture works let's imagine a simple scenario of having to make choices: looking at the menu of a pizza restaurant. This menu reveals only three items of food

Pizza; Pasta; Salad.

These printed menu items, by a process of depiction (ax1) and attention (ax2) become, in turn (say), the states of the perceptual neural module, **P**. These act as inputs to the memory/imagination module **M**. Now, it is in this module that the 'thinking' goes on. In this case the thinking has to do with imagining the action that might be taken: eating pizza, pasta or salad. But this is not all one imagines. One recalls the taste of these dishes, and a whole lot of emotions associated with them. This and the operation of the emotion module **E**, needs some elaboration.

The emotion process

Emotions are taken to have the following character: first, they are remembered in the context of a predicted action and result of that action. For example, in imagining in **M** the action of eating pizza, I remember the result of this (the taste) and I also remember the associated emotions. That is, it is the presence of the action state, the taste state and the emotion states that make up the total state of **M**. There could be several emotions states present at the same time: say, a gustatory pleasure, and also guilt because this is bad for my weight. That is, the predicted result of an action can have a collection of emotions associated with it, some positive and some negative. The second character of emotions is that they have a value, that is, an intensity, a strength with which an outcome is wanted. Third, under normal conditions, it is possible to resolve unclear combinations of emotions and make decisions in any case.

In the model we are here developing, the role of the **E** module is to recognise the imagined emotion and to evaluate it, that is to create a value of 'wantedness'. This is not an instantaneous process and may involve attending to the available actions several times. The feeling is a familiar one: it takes a while to ponder the content of a menu so the predicted actions and their results are visited several times. Whenever a choice of action is visited in **M**, the total of all the related emotional values is summed up to give a 'how much wanted' value for each action.

So, in our emotional model, **E** generates a signal **z** when a sufficient level of wantedness is achieved. This is fed back to the imagination/memory module and holds that module in the action that has given rise to this high level. At the same time this signal is also sent to the action module enabling it to be set up to drive muscles as required by the action that is currently in **M** that the organism has decided to take. Of course this scheme allows for the **E** module never to reach an adequate 'wanting' intensity. To deal with this and conflicting or unclear decisions implies that in **E** there should be some of Epicurus' 'swerves'. In modern science this would be called a random process. The object of the random process is to provide an arbitrary enhancement of the 'wantedness' score in such a way that higher scores are more likely to trigger the action, but that lower score can also achieve this but with a lower likelihood. Even where there is no wantedness, just through the need to make an arbitrary decision (as in Libet's experiments) the random process can make the arbitrary decision of *when* to act.

Neural swerves

Neural networks are very good at random processes, and it is often assumed that the neural structures of the brain are capable of this. In Fig. 6.2 below, a simulated ten-neuron net that has not been trained on anything is shown producing a sequence of four arbitrary patterns.

Were these patterns treated as intensities (by counting the number of firing [black] neurons, this random process is seen to generate the sequence of values 5, 4, 5, 3. In fact, with a random process like this, the probability of generating a particular value

Figure 6.2   A 10-neuron net with no training shown producing a sequence of four arbitrary patterns.

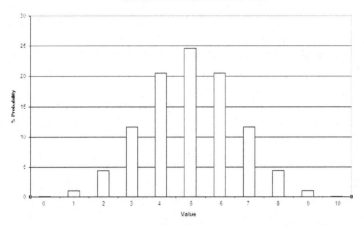

Figure 6.3 The expected probability with which the 10-neuron net generates given values. Numerically these are 0 and 10 = .097%, 1 and 9 = 0.97%, 8 and 2 = 4. 4% , 7 and 3 = 11.7%, 6 and 4 = 20.5%, 5 = 24.6%.

can be calculated using a so-called binomial distribution. This is shown for the 10-neuron net in fig. 6.3.

This can be interpreted as saying that, if asked 100 times the net will generate, say, the value 5 just under 25 times on average. Or, about 1 in 4 times the value will be 5, while the value 8 will occur only about once in about 25 times (having a probability of about 4%). The extreme values such as 0 and 10 have a probability of about 0.1 % hence are not expected to crop up more often than about once in 1000 times.

Now we can go back to the example and list the emotional value that might be in force at one particular moment that our organism is trying to decide what to eat. This can be set out as a table :

Menu Item	Taste Pleasure	Lack of Guilt	Total Value (Emotional)
Pizza	3	0	3
Pasta	2	0	2
Salad	1	1	2

Now say that to make a decision (generate signal **z**) the **E** machinery has to equal or exceed a value of 7 when adding the total emotional value to that of the random process net. So, the decision for pizza will be made when the **M** module is in the Pizza state and the random process generates 4 or more. This is obtained by adding the probabilities of random values from 4 to 10 all of which will cause the action. This sum turns out to be 82.8%. Similarly, when **M** is "thinking" of Pasta or Salad the random process must generate a value of at least 5. Summing the probabilities of generating 5 or greater indicates that the decision to eat the dish currently thought of, will be taken in 62.3% cases.

A way of interpreting these results is to think of 100 (99 to be precise to have a number divisible by 3) people in this restaurant. They all have exactly the same feelings about the three dishes and each has the same random process. Each will be in one of the three food states, say about a third (33) in each. So of the group thinking 'pizza' (0.828x99/3) will make their decision to eat pizza that is, about 28 will make a firm decision to eat pizza. We note that 5 will make no decision at all, and return to consider the next item on the menu. Similarly, of the other two groups of 33 about 20 will choose pasta in the pasta group and 20 will choose salad in the salad group.

Of course these figures depend on the threshold of 7 that has been chosen to do the calculations. Had a higher threshold been chosen, the restaurant clients would be seen to be far less prepared to make decisions. So this threshold can be seen as a sort of 'mood' emotion. A hungry, relaxed mood (low threshold) will lead to a quick decision whereas, an anxious, picky mood (high threshold) will cause the organism to agonise longer before taking a decision.

The point of all this is to show that uncertainties and conflicting emotional values *could* be represented in machinery as shown in fig.6.1. I stress that it is not the case that this precise machinery is thought to exist in human brains. It is more an expression of the axiomatic stance which suggests that an architecture might at least be envisaged which appears to have the characteristics of emotional evaluations that go on in my head when I am trying to make a decision. But this needs a bit more discussion.

How does it feel?

The main tenet of the axiomatic approach is that only that which is depicted is experienced as a meaningful sensation. In figure 6.1 only the **P** and the **M** modules are depictive, **P**, directly and **M** indirectly as a memory of the states in **P**. Therefore it is quite true to say that we are fully conscious of what our options are and the nature of the emotion that comes with them. I have argued in chapter 2 that some such feelings are 'wired in' as, for example, fear, pain and pleasure are internally generated neural signals the reach the depictive areas in order to come into consciousness as 'visceral' sensations.

What is new here is that I have imagined a little further than in the Appendix how the emotion module could use a random process to control the generation of action in situations where a direct reactive response (such as swiping my hand at a fly that has settled on my nose) is not possible due to there being several choices. While this process is not in the depictive part of the mechanism and I would not be conscious of it, the generation of **z** comes into consciousness as it holds the state of **M** for long enough to transfer the imagined action to the action module. This 'freezing' is what we would describe as the moment of consciousness that a particular action would be taken. This now puts us into a position where we can re-visit Libet's findings, and decide that perhaps will is not an illusion after all.

Lifting Libet's finger

In Libet's experimental setting, the decision to be made is not 'what' but 'when'. While there may be thoughts and emotions present about what one is meant to do, they do not have a direct bearing on the process. I suggest that the only thing that remains at work is the random process. Everything in the **M** module is set up to lift the finger, that is the intention is depicted, but the random 'wanting' machinery is on its own as there are no emotions to evaluate. In such a situation the threshold for generating **z** should be within the range of values produced by the random process on its own. For the sake of an explanation, we assume that the same random process is at work and this means that the threshold 7 will be reached if the random process produces **z** with the sum of the probabilities of generating 7, 8, 9 and 10. Just out of interest this turns out to be 17.2%, that is, somewhat lower than the 'choice' restaurant decisions in which emotions are evaluated.

It is now possible to create a hypothesis that makes the unconscious generation of the Readiness Potential less mysterious and will less of an illusion. First, I submit that the generation of something like **z** in **E** *is* the readiness potential. But this is not the source of the willed action, just an emotion-like trigger that the action should take place. So it is hardly surprising that this trigger should be generated before the depiction of the action in **M** freezes, which is the moment at which the participant knows what she wants and looks at the clock.

In other words the sequence of events goes like this: the desire to lift the finger at some point is fully depicted in **M**, but without input from **E**. This activates the random process which with some delay determined by the probability (i.e. not the same each time) of exceeding the threshold, generates **z** (the readiness potential) to which **M** reacts, say, half a second later and the action is transferred to the muscles a little while after that. But there seems little doubt to me that it is the initial desire depicted in **M** that is the cause of these events. It now becomes possible to summarise this perspective of the concept of will that has been developed in this chapter.

Will: a summary

The beginning of this chapter pointed to the simple way that we feel our own volition — we visualise something we desire — we act to get it. But our cultural inheritance from philosophy and religion and some recent neurological measurements would not leave it at that. Important questions have to be answered, and here I attempt to summarise what might have been gleaned through the depictive approach.

The first of the important questions is that of *freedom*. In what sense can the system in fig. 6.1 convey the notion of freedom? More pertinently, say that some elaborate form of this system were present in my brain, how is it that it makes me *feel* free to make my decisions in an unfettered way? I suggest that this freedom is felt at least at two levels. Back in the pizza restaurant scenario, I know, as I can know anything else, that in going to the restaurant, I shall be offered a choice of food on which I will be able to exercise my power of choice, with its emotional overtones. This is knowledge like any other: like knowing that when I go into my study I will find a computer on the desk or like knowing that when I go to Venice I will have to leave my car in a garage outside the watery city. All this is due to the natural mechanistic implications of axiom 2: areas such as **M** provide access to knowledge and experience, and my knowledge of restaurants tells me that I will be able to make a choice that suits me at the time, dependent on my moods and emotions.

Of course, someone could say that it is all written in the stars. But it does not *feel* that way just because I am aware of having made different choices under similar conditions. So, written in the stars or not, the feeling that what I will choose, that which will be best for me at the time, is good enough not to feel constrained. What would *not* feel free would be the prediction from my prison cell that the same slop as always will arrive at midday. Oh for the choice of three dishes on the pizza restaurant menu!

The above is the first, higher, level of feeling the freedom of will. The second, lower, level, is the mechanism of evaluating emotional states for a series of attentional phases directed (say) at the restaurant menu. The cycling and eventual freezing of the state all occur in **M**, which, according to the depictive axioms, is felt by the organism. Given language and choice of the most wanted item, the organism would describe this sensation as 'I felt free to look at the choices offered on the menu and chose the one that appealed to me most'. Or if a less wanted item was chosen this might be described as 'I chose salad despite the fact that I don't like it all that much, but I know is good for me'. In the finger lifting exercise I would admit that I didn't know what made me lift a finger at a particular time and that that moment seemed arbitrary to me.

The second question about what factors influence my choice is answered by the way I have suggested that emotional evalua- tions work. Emotions are recalled in **M** and the factors of 'wantedness' are computed in **E**. Of course this process has not been fully elaborated here and is the subject of current research. Open questions relate to how the evaluations get developed through learning and how 'thresholds' develop and change with moods. Finally, the mechanisms described here clarify the involvement of axiom 4 and 5 as the basis of free will. Axiom 4 is the cycling in **M** and axiom 5 is the operation of the **E** machinery.

Will: a philosophical coda

While mechanistic arguments have been heavily employed in the last few paragraphs above, philosophers may not be happy with this. I conclude this chapter by setting out the logic of the argument in a series of assertions.

For an organism with a 'brain' to have a sensation of free will:

1. There exist areas of the brain that support consciousness through having the depictive property (axioms 1 & 2)

2. There exists in the brain a depictive mechanism for cycling through the choices prompted by a perceived external event or an internal imagined event.

3. Cycling through the states in 2 includes memories of emo- tions associated with the choice states.

4. There exists in the brain a non-depictive evaluational mechanism (non-conscious, that is) that accumulates 'wantedness' values for the emotions associated with each choice. When wantedness exceeds some threshold the cur- rent choice state is translated into action.

5. As part of the evaluational mechanism, there exists a ran- dom process which adds to the wantedness values helping to resolve situations of conflict or lack of emotional value.

6. Through the depiction of the freezing of the cycling mecha- nism due to a wantedness trigger, the organism feels that

actions are taken among choices according to how much something is wanted.

Conditions 1 and 2 are fundamental postulates which, if denied, block proceeding with the rest. Denying 3 requires a denial that emotions are involved in making choices. Such a denial would contradict common experience. 4 and 5 are then the basis of the main hypothesis presented here, their denial or confirmation is a matter for both neurological and modelling research.

Chapter 7

Chalmers' Two Minds

The problem of consciousness may not be all that hard

Health warning: this chapter is written in some detail to satisfy those who have followed or would like to follow David Chalmers' reasoning about the impossibility of understanding the 'hard' problem of consciousness from a physical or material standpoint. It also contains my refutation of this argument without which this book would not make sense. But this is detailed philosophical stuff. The reader who wants to get on with the concluding part of the book can simply skip the entire chapter.

David Chalmers has become one of the most influential philosophers among those who would like to 'explain' consciousness.[1] His fame stems from having produced a sophisticated argument for his belief that while there is an almost direct correlation between the materialistic operation of the brain and what we experience as sensation , there is still a gulf between the two. The material side can be tackled by conventional neurological or cognitive science while no existing science can tackle the experiential side. He has called the first of these 'easy' and the second 'hard'. While this is often hailed as a historical contribution to the power of latter-day dualism, I (among others) feel that there is a reading of Chalmers' reasoning that accords with the informational models in this book. This

---

[1]   Chalmers, D. J. (1996), *The Conscious Mind: In Search of a Fundamental Theory* (New York: Oxford University Press).

is just as well as the 'gap' is in complete contrast to what I am attempting to establish with this book. That is, that an understanding of mechanism is fundamental and getting rid of mysteries rather than creating strange explanatory gaps is what needs to be done. In this chapter I set out David Chalmers' argument (recommending the interested reader to read the original) interspersed with comments on where there is and where there isn't accord with the axiomatic, depictive point of view.

David Chalmers

David Chalmers' undergraduate education was rigorously rooted in Mathematics and Computer Science at the University of Adelaide in Australia. I have known many philosophers who have sought the refuge of a safe science by moving *into* mathematics and computing where David Chalmers is moving in the opposite direction. After a brief graduate spell at the University of Oxford as a mathematician he not only crossed the Atlantic pond to complete his PhD in Indiana University, but also crossed the intellectual ocean with a PhD thesis in Philosophy and Cognitive Science. A fellowship at the University of Washington and then a few years in the department of Philosophy at the University of California at Santa Cruz then took him to be Professor of Philosophy and Director of the Center for Consciousness studies at the University of Arizona. At the time of writing he has just returned home to take up a similar appontment at the Australian National University in Canberra. I met him once or twice at conferences: he speaks straight, asks direct questions and is clearly an authority that is hard to cross. Because he develops his arguments with logical force, I look at his point of view in some detail.

The hard problem remains untouched

Right at the beginning of Chalmers' celebrated book *The Conscious Mind: In Search of a Fundamental Theory*, he clarifies his position. Great progress has been made in the neurosciences and psychology in providing scientific ways of talking about the mind but, despite this he goes on to say, 'Consciousness, however, is as perplexing as it ever was.' Admittedly the brain is a huge information processing machine, responsible for astonishingly complex behaviour. But understanding these mechanisms does not answer what for Chalmers is the central question: 'Why is all this processing accompanied by an experienced inner life?'

This leads to two aspects of mind: the psychological (or mechanistic/informational) and the phenomenological (or inner/ experiential). In Chalmers' philosophy these need to be kept separate.[2]

> *So, right from the beginning, the fact that Chalmers talks of an inner life as **accompanying** the material action of the brain, the experiential inner life is presented as an addendum to the smooth working of a behaving information processing organism. We begin to sense that he believes that the organism could just as easily behave and survive without having this inner life.*
>
> *Chalmers despairs of people like me who argue that explanations in the psychological or neurological domain actually cross over into the phenomenological one. He sees this as the confusion of two separate concepts. As we progress through this chapter I shall argue that the new dualism between psychological and phenomenological explanation is as arbitrary an assumption as assuming that the two are the same.*

The methodology of supervenience

To avoid arguments about the meaning of phrases such as 'the physical *causes* the phenomenological' Chalmers introduces the relationship of supervenience: property B *supervenes* on property A if, whenever one meets A, one can be sure of finding B. For example property A could be 'H_2O at room temperature' and B could be 'a clear flowing liquid'. In broad principle, finding pure H_2O at room temperature usually accompanies the presence of a clear flowing liquid (as opposed to, say, some green slimy gloop).

The above example is what might be called a *natural* supervenience, dictated by the physics of the situation. There is also the possibility of a *logical* supervenience which is key to

---

[2] In this section I shall be paraphrasing Chalmers' ideas in normal font, interposing my comments *in indented italics*.

Chalmers' argument. B supervenes logically on A if for every situation that A occurs, one logically (that is, not necessarily evoking scientific laws, just the conventions of logic) expects B to be true. For example, a flying pig may be logically possible despite being physically hard. On some other planet pigs may well have wings. So 'not being able to fly' supervenes naturally but not logically on the fact 'pig'. In contrast, the fact 'impossible' supervenes logically on ' integer X is both odd and even'.

If B is *not* logically supervenient on A one cannot have a scientific explanation of B in terms of A. It is a waste of time to try to prove logically that pigs cannot fly. Central to Chalmers' argument is that consciousness is not logically supervenient on the physical facts about the brain and therefore any brain science does not point to unique facts about being conscious. He argues this in five ways.

1. The logical possibility of zombies

It is often said that the only consciousness of which we can be absolutely sure is our own. So as we cannot be sure that anyone else is conscious we must allow that they may not be despite their conscious-like behaviour. The mere fact that this is a situation that has been exploited in science fiction literature, indicates that it is logically possible to conceive of such zombies. A story of a world where an integer could be both odd and even, would be labelled as uninteresting as it offends the sense of logic of the reader. A story about zombies holds no such offence.

In a subtle way, Chalmers is drawing attention to the fact that the concept of consciousness is not logically sown up. As we cannot logically rule out the possibility of a zombie means that starting with the physical which could be common both to conscious and non-conscious organisms we cannot achieve an explanation of consciousness.

> *While not directly flawed, the argument that consciousness does not supervene logically on the physical, for me, leads to a conclusion which is different from saying that the physical cannot be 'linked' to consciousness. The lack of logical supervenience is merely a 'don't know' situation. I can't know*

whether my neighbour is conscious. This does not mean that I have to deny my own consciousness. As, through neuroscience, I know something about my physical makeup I can legitimately attempt to link the two. It is for this reason that I have insisted that any axiomatic theory of being conscious needs to be intro- spective. Were it to happen that a neat theory emerges from this approach and that it works in my case, it becomes open to any- one else who thinks they are conscious to check the theory intro- spectively. Should zombies exist, as they are devoid of consciousness, hence introspection , they will not be able to do anything with the theory.

Is this just another psychological rather than phenomeno- logical approach? Not at all! The approach starts with a need to discover mechanisms that could support the phenomenology, the crossing link being the 'locking' and 'depiction' actually found in the brain as discussed in chapter 2.

2. The inverted spectrum

Chalmers recognises the somewhat extreme nature of the 'zom- bie world' argument and provides a softer route to the belief that consciousness does not logically supervene on physical brain action. This simply draws on the logical possibility that differing conscious organisms, could derive a different type of conscious- ness from the same physical substrate. As an example he cites two physically identical organisms who have inverted colour experiences with respect to one another.

He asks us to imagine two identically wired twins with inverted colour sensations. When blue is being observed, twin A has the appropriate blue sensation but twin B has a red sensa- tion. When red happens, again A has the 'right' sensation and B the opposite one.

There are many flaws in this argument, but the principal one is that what is to be concluded (that consciousness is not logically supervenient on the physical) is built into the way that the inverted spectrum argument has been couched. It is assumed in the argument that 'a blue experience' and 'a red experience' have a logically possible existence simultaneously in the two identical individuals. This is tantamount to saying that colour experience is not supervenient on physical events. It would be just as easy to argue that whatever is meant by 'a red experience' or a 'blue experience' cannot coexist in two organisms, identical or not, as, in the presence of a blue world, whatever the experience in these individuals is, it cannot be labelled in any other way than a 'blue experience'. So this is as logically impossible as an integer being odd and even at the same time.

Now, it could be that the state of the physical apparatus in A for blue is the same as the state of the physical apparatus in B for red. This can happen despite the identical wiring of the two organisms as the history of states (i.e. the experience) of the two can be quite different. But calling these two states a blue experience and a red experience as some fundamental definition is a nonsense. A theoretical link between the conscious experience of A and the world of colours is exactly the same as that of B and the world of colours even if the states are different.

If the argument is pushed to saying that both organisms are in the same state but could logically have different experiences is a repetition of the non-supervenience belief, making light work of the point that there is no logical way in which the first person experience of two organisms in identical states could be compared.

3: From epistemic asymmetry

The route by which we get to know about consciousness (that is, its epistemic foundation) is undoubtedly different from the route that we get to know about any other thing. Chalmers points out that we can infer most things that we know from the physical makeup of the world. For example, even in ancient Greece, Thales of Miletus, in the sixth century BC was able to predict the coming of solar eclipses and good harvests from astronomical observation. But, says Chalmers, no amount of observation of the physical world predicts that some organisms should be conscious. This creates an imbalance between the way consciousness needs to be understood and the way that anything else needs to be understood. This, he argues, is proof that consciousness does not logically supervene on the physical.

It is the last of the above statements that does not exactly follow the previous ones. Yes, of course knowing I am conscious has an internal character whereas noticing an eclipse has an external character. But this does not mean that both should not logically supervene on some physical substrate. The argument that start-

*ing with the physical one cannot predict that organisms can be
conscious is also not logically sound. There are many abstract
areas of physics that did not emerge directly just from external
information about the world: quantum systems being the most
obvious. The fact that being conscious is epistemically unusual
does not mean that it is divorced from the physical.*

*The axioms of Chapter 2 indicate a way in which an organism
can be physically considered to predict whether it could be conscious. This is not all that different from providing a molecular
analysis of a material to predict whether it can or cannot con-
duct electricity.*

4. The knowledge argument

Here Chalmers turns to a well trodden example created by
Frank Jackson in 1982[3]. This is the celebrated story of the unfortunate Mary whom some cruel scientists had brought up in a
colourless environment. In revenge she becomes acquainted
with what by then had become a completely worked out science
of how the brain works. The upshot of this is that no matter how
clever Mary is in understanding how the brain gets into different
states for red and blue, if shown a coloured object, Mary would
not know if it was red or blue. According to Chalmers, "It follows that the facts about the subjective experience of colour
vision are not entailed by the physical facts."

*I am not the only one to point out that if her knowledge was
sound she would predict that she could not have a colour sensation as nothing in her brain had adapted to distinguish colours.
But if her theory is so good as to predict from a knowledge of the
structure and state of someone's brain that this person is having
(say) what they would call a red sensation, that would be good
enough for me. In a highly tentative way this is what the axioms
of the chapter 2 are for: they aim to draw attention to what needs
to be happening in a brain-like mechanism for that mechanism
to be responsible for a sensation.*

Supporters of the Mary argument point out that if Mary were
to be shown red and blue objects for the first time and told what

---

[3]   Jackson, F. (1982), 'Epiphenomenal qualia', *Philosophical Quarterly*, **32**,
      127–136.

they are she will have learned something new — ostensibly with no change in the physical structure of her brain.

> *But it is obvious that some new cells will have been stimulated in Mary's brain as colour is revealed and colours are distinguished. What has been learned has a physical support so this provides no currency to sustain the argument that sensation does not supervene logically on the physical.*

5. From the absence of analysis

Chalmers' final argument against the physical entailing consciousness is the most direct — nobody has analysed consciousness to show that it breaks down into physical action. All attempts fail because one cannot use physical arguments that add up to 'a certain phenomenal feel'.

> *No one doubts that phenomenal feel cannot be classified as a physical event and hence be the outcome of a physical analysis. But neither can the reflection of an object in a mirror. And yet the physical is sufficient for us to understand everything that needs to be known about the reflected virtual image in the mirror. That is, we can say that certain conditions need to be satisfied for the reflection to exist: a certain smoothness of the reflecting surface, certain lighting conditions, and so on. Having understood these conditions leaves no mysteries to be solved to understand images in mirrors. This is precisely the argument implied in the five axioms: what physical conditions need to be present for the phenomenal feel to be possible? The brain is more complicated than a mirror, so the scale of the analytic operation is much greater, but not logically unavailable. The trick to understanding how organisms can be conscious has to do with scaling these heights of complexity and the five axioms are just the first few steps.*

Cognitive models do not do the trick

In a sense, Chalmers' supervenience methodology is only a primer on his attack on material explanations. He would argue that my five axioms are 'cognitive models' rather than explanations of conscious experience. Cognitive models explain the working of psychological processes such as '… learning, mem-

ory, perception, control of action, attention, categorization, linguistic behaviour and so on'. This does indeed sound like the
five axioms. But, argues Chalmers, having good models
whether functional or material does not explain why the realisation of the model should be 'accompanied by consciousness'.

> *So here again, lies the assumption that consciousness is some-
> thing separate – something that accompanies the model. My
> contention is that it is just another aspect of the model. Making
> more use of the reflection in the mirror analogy, were I to explain
> why a ball is bouncing on a smooth surface, I need do no more to
> explain the 'accompanying' image of the bouncing ball in the
> mirror (having once explained what mirrors do). Therefore it
> may be quite true that the five axioms relate to cognitive events,
> but then, what is consciousness but a complex interplay of cog-
> nitive events? Explaining the conscious planning in the control
> of one's next action cannot be divorced from what is known
> about action control gleaned from cognitive models. An even
> more powerful drive for cognitive modelling is to learn to design
> models that may support consciousness against models that
> may not as attempted in the five axioms.*

Chalmers cites several examples of cognitive models to demonstrate that they do not lead to an understanding of consciousness. He mentions Baars' Global Workspace model (see Chapter
1) but criticises it because it does not contain anything that could
be argued gives rise to conscious experience: it just behaves in a
competent way. Cognitive models that have been produced by
the likes of Dennett[4] and many others (boxes and arrows models) are criticised in the same way: they may explain complex
behaviours but do not tell us why consciousness arises in the
organisms that are being modelled.

> *At this point it could be said that Chalmers' attack is directed at
> 'functional' models. As explained in chapter 2these are more
> concerned with the rules of computational behaviour rather
> than the than the actual operation of brain mechanisms. Not so!
> Neurobiological explanations are next in line for disembowel-
> ment.*

---

[4]   Dennett, D.C. (1991), *Consiousness Explained* (London: Allen Lane).

How does the brain do it?

The main substance of Chalmers' attack is that those who develop theories based on neurobiology, themselves deny that these neurobiological explanations include consciousness. For some time now Francis Crick and Christof Koch have led the field in this area with neurological explanations of (for example) the binding of different components of (say) a visual sensation (see also Chapter 2). In this work the authors have drawn a distinction between subjective feelings and awareness. They claim to address awareness and not the way subjective feelings arise. Indeed they write of the 'Neural Correlates of Consciousness' giving Chalmers the ammunition to pick on the word 'correlate': 'They can also tell us something about the brain processes that are *correlated* with consciousness ... But none of these accounts explains the correlation ... From the point of view of neuroscience the correlation is simply a brute fact.'[5]

> *I do think that the use of the word 'correlation' is unfortunate. In a sense it sinks Francis Crick's 'Astonishing Hypothesis'[6] that our consciousness is precisely the working of the brain which, when fully understood, will leave little else to be discovered about the nature of being conscious. This is precisely my standpoint: personal sensation implies some brain activity and this brain activity implies the personal sensation. This, in mathematics is not a correlation it is an identity, as seen in chapter 2.*

Materialism is false (or is it?)

To recap, a materialist like myself is someone who believes that being conscious does logically supervene on the physical and that accounting for the physical is what is needed to account for being conscious. Chalmers has a numbered attack:

1. In our world there are conscious experiences.

---

[5]   Crick F and Koch C (1998), 'Consciousness and neuroscience', *Cereb Cortex*, **8** (2), 97–107.
[6]   Crick, F.H.C. (1994), *The Astonishing Hypothesis* (London: Simon and Schuster).

2. There is a logically possible world physically identical to ours, in which the positive facts about consciousness in our world do not hold.

3. Therefore, facts about consciousness are further facts about our world, over and above the physical facts.

4. So, materialism is false.

I would certainly not dispute point 1. However, throughout this chapter, I have argued that 2 is an assumption which simply stems from the belief that materialism is false. Assume that I have developed a relatively watertight materialist theory that identifies 'every scrap' of internal sensation with detailed brain mechanisms, this would contain a theorem which states that if all the mechanisms are in place, the organism will be conscious. The believer in point 2 would then have produce evidence that falsifies my theory — he would have to produce evidence of the actual existence of zombie worlds. Their 'logical possibility' is merely a literary device. If I could produce a materialist theory that applies to the world we actually live in and the consciousness I know so intimately, this might be too valuable to be overthrown by a literary device.

The key challenge for the materialist, therefore, is to be convincing about the identity between the physical and the phenomenological. Like the image in the mirror, it has an identity with the object that generates it and the materialist theory of objects suffices to predict everything the image will do. So point 4 might read: materialism is still alive and well.

A non-reductive theory

So far it would seem as if all that Chalmers has done is to be negative about materialistic or reductive theories of being conscious. But half way through the book one discovers the focus of his contribution: the possibility of a *non-reductive* theory.

Here Chalmers concentrates on what he calls the *natural* supervenience of consciousness on the physical and that this can lead to a set of *psychophysical* laws that relate consciousness to physical systems.

Given the physical facts about a system such laws will enable us to infer what sort of conscious experience will be associated with the system, if any.

Coherence

Suddenly there appears to be mounting agreement between Chalmers' narrative and the approach to theory advocated in this book. But rather than to speak of an *identity* between the physical and the phenomenological, Chalmers speaks of *coherence*: 'The most promising way to get started in developing a theory of consciousness is to focus on the remarkable *coherence* between conscious experience and cognitive structure.'

> *Cognitive structure is the material of the axioms : out-there perceptions, imagination, attention, foresight and emotional control of thought.*

Chalmers also uses the word *awareness* to describe the internal physical state that carries cognitive information and sees the above coherence as extending to consciousness *and* awareness. Interestingly, he agrees the bi-directional relationship between the two: 'So far we have a hypothesis: where there is consciousness there is awareness and where there is (the right kind of) awareness, there is consciousness.' He goes on to speak of a *structural coherence*, for example: 'My visual field consists in a mass of details, which fit together into an encompassing structure.'

This points to the fact that there must be a link between the structure of conscious events (like feeling that there is a solid world out there) and the physical events that could support this feeling. This is a vague pointer to axiom 1: the depictive nature of perception.

Organizational invariance

Another major point of agreement between the axioms and Chalmers' non-reductive ideas is indicated by: 'I will argue for a *principle of organizational invariance,* holding that given any system that has conscious experiences, then any system that has the same fine-grained functional organisation will have qualitatively identical experiences.'

> *This is a robust endorsement of the need for fine-grain structure (such as neural structure that reflects what is known in neurol-*

*ogy) in machines that model consciousness. This implies that
non-biological conscious systems can exist provided that they
have the right fine-grained structure.*

Consciousness and information

Chalmers suggests that the above non-reductive theories (coherence between awareness and consciousness, structural coherence and organisational invariance) might be just the components of a final theory. Chalmers suggests that many further questions need to be answered to complement the above principles. In common with the outlook of this book, one salient question is what kind of mechanism could give raise to the above three principles. It is precisely with a view to specifying such mechanisms that the five axioms of this book were derived. For me to be convinced that an organism is conscious, I need to find mechanisms which plausibly do the work that is indicated by the axioms.

Again, in common with some principles I have outlined elsewhere,[7,8] Chalmers has drawn attention to some relevant properties of information processing systems, which may point in the direction of further theoretical constructs of being conscious. He refers to an 'information space' where I might use the words 'state space' from the tradition of the field of automata theory (See Appendix). An information space or a state space is the space of all the possible states that a cellular physical system could acquire. For example, a system of three neurons each of which can either fire or not has a space of precisely eight states. Brains with their large numbers of neurons have immensely vast state spaces according to the relationship (number of states) = 2 to the power of (number of neurons). So 3 neurons have 8 states, but even 30 neurons have approximately 10,000,000,000 states.

Within these spaces, specific conscious activities correspond either to specific states or sequences of such states (called state space trajectories). Chalmers puts this as: " ... when an experi-

[7] Aleksander, I. (1996), *Impossible Minds: My Consciousness, My Neurons.* (London: Imperial College Press).
[8] Aleksander, I. (2001), *How to Build a Mind: Machines with Imagination.* (London: Phoenix Paperbacks).

ence realizes an information state the same information state is realised in the experience's physical substrate." I shall comment on these points of agreement later, now it might be worth returning briefly to the question of the hard problem and the reaction of the consciousness-seeking community to Chalmers' ideas.

The critics

The material of the next few sections is all drawn from a compilation of comments on the hard problem edited by Jonathan Shear of the Department of Philosophy at Virginia Commonwealth University.[9] This work was triggered by asking eminent commentators on consciousness how they reacted to Chalmers' notion of the 'hard problem' as having to be treated as a non-physical phenomenon demanding a novel and as yet ill-defined science.

Deflationary Perspectives

A group of critics opens the discussion in a direct way by deflating the 'hard problem' argument either by arguing that it is analogous to other cognitive elements or that sectoring it out as 'special' is merely an arbitrary matter of preference.

The first in the line of attack is Daniel Dennett. He queries Chalmers' suggestion that the way to deal with the hard problem is to recognise that 'experience' should be treated as a fundamental phenomenon. This, like mass, charge and space-time in physics requires to be accepted as being the basis for a science rather than attempting to define it in terms of other, as yet, unclear elements. Dennett argues that this is an arbitrary claim that requires independent reasons to support it rather than being just stated as a belief. Without such support why should anyone give it any consideration? In light hearted vein he refers to 'cutism' (being 'cute') as being as detached from physical function as experience, but not demanding a new science to explain it.

[9]   Shear, J., ed. (1995), *Explaining Consciousness: The Hard Problem* (Cambridge, MA: MIT Press).

> *There is a way in which I actually side with Chalmers under*
> *Dennett's attack. As reflected in the axioms, I do believe that it is*
> *possible to treat personal experience as a fundamental starting*
> *point in the development of a theory and ask questions about*
> *what possible mechanisms could support it. This introspective*
> *approach would be an entirely unique process which 'cuteness'*
> *would not require. No need for independent grounds, just treat*
> *the fundamental nature of experience as a postulate and see how*
> *far it gets you.*

Patricia Churchland, a philosopher of the University of California at San Diego, points out that at any point in the history of science it is not possible to predict which problems cannot be temporarily solved and which require some sort of scientific revolution. Therefore Chalmers' claiming a special status for experience as being a fundamental element that stands apart from neuroscientific investigation may be premature. Natural development of a study of physical mechanisms might still be shown to be directly responsible for experience. Churchland cites many other 'hard' problems in the neurosciences: schizophrenia and autism. Neuroscientists have not found sound neural processes that underpin these deficits. Treating these as *fundamental* would be tantamount to abandoning just the neuroscientific research routes that might help those afflicted by these problems.

> *This squares up with the axiomatic approach of chapter 2 in the*
> *sense that the axioms suggest important mechanisms from*
> *which the development of such a study might start. In chapter 8*
> *we shall see how these axioms provide pointers to research on*
> *mental deficits.*

Thomas Clark, a moralist philosopher, among others points out that understanding is served by assuming that experience may be approached from a standpoint of being part of a natural world that can be explained by physics, biology or information theory. Choosing to define a 'hard problem' is a matter of philosophical preference which may not serve progress. He stresses that the latter parts of Chalmers' philosophy (various aspects of coherence) point in the direction that the physical and the experiential are identical to one another.

The counterpounch so far

Chalmers took the opportunity to reply to his critics and, in the case of Dennett and Churchland pointed out that their examples such as 'cuteness' on the one hand, and badly understood areas of neurophysiology are not analogous to the distinctive hard problem of consciousness as they do not exclude a functional basis. What makes people cute is something psychologists have fun explaining and the fact that schizophrenia is being studied by experiment and theory has hopes for a functional solution. According to Chalmers one of the reasons that the hard problem is distinctive is precisely because it appears to have no functional analogues. Chalmers sticks to his guns that losing the distinction between physical or psychological objects and consciousness will lead to inappropriate explanations.

As many perspectives as commentators?

Jonathan Shear's book is important as it places Chalmers' views against the background of approaches extant in the mid 1990s. There are several 'camps'. The first camp are those who are concerned that some of the 'hardness' of the hard problem has not entered Chalmers' assessment. Colin McGinn of Rutgers University in the US homes in on the fact that experience such as that of a yellow flash may not be localised in the world but localised in the brain. The two do not 'cohere' perhaps in the way that Chalmers suggests they might. Eugene Mills a philosopher at the Virginia Commonwealth University goes further to suggest that not only is the problem hard, but that Chalmers has not been convincing that a 'non reductive' theory of coherence and information might ever scale the heights of this hardness.

A group that includes Roger Penrose and Stuart Hamerhoff highlight quantum physics as not fitting into oversimplified ways of thinking of 'physical' explanations of consciousness. It provides a physical way of analysing consciousness. This is followed by views from the neurosciences led by Francis Crick and Christof Koch. They argue that the neurosciences are the best place to get insights of how the physical controls the experiential.

A further group claim to re-think nature. What William Seager means by this is that 'panpsychism' (all matter and all nature having a mental basis) taken in the sense of being 'informational' is a perspective that avoids the explanatory gap. That is, they agree with Chalmers that the duality between the physical structure of an informational system and it's 'state' structure provides an analytic lead to the body-mind relationship. The final group of papers is entitled 'First person Perspectives' and contains a contribution by Max Velmans of Goldsmiths College in London University who partly agrees with Chalmers. He interprets the separation between the physical and the experiential as a 'dual-aspect' theory where the two are manifestations of something more fundamental than either. He disagrees on some definitions and points out that for some, 'awareness' and 'consciousness' are interchangeable where for Chalmers they represent the two ends of the physical/experiential dichotomy. In general, he feels that Chalmers is being too rigorous in his beliefs in coherence and organizational invariance.

The Final Response

As might be expected Chalmers defends both his 'hard problem' definition and his ideas of a path towards a non-reductive theory. He concludes that progress towards a theory is a route where, at specific points, choices are to be made. Examples are whether the experiential is distinguished from the physical, whether the two form an identity and what is the nature of possible psychophysical laws. He sees his critics as making different choices from himself but sees that progress is a question of clarifying the consequences of these choices and the reasoning that underpins them.

Whither the axioms?

The approach I have taken in this book is curious in one particular way: it starts with the phenomenological side of the divide. When others do this, the phenomenology is brought into the dicussion largely as the reports of a person being tested, for example: stimulate a nerve and ask the participant what she feels. So the conventional flow tends to be from stimulus to reported sensation. I am advocating that this should be done the other way around. Starting with the class of my own personal experience (such as the visual experience of the world out there), I take seriously what Chalmers says about the informational nature of a possible theory and ask what possible physical structures could have internal states that are like the ones that I am experiencing.

Significantly this cuts out arguments about zombie worlds. Were zombies to exist they would not be able to contemplate their own experience and perform the first person science that I am advocating. Many of the arguments of non supervenience of consciousness on the material brain fall away. If we are to understand what it is to be conscious, I suggest starting with conscious experiences and, as an exercise in synthesis, ask what it is about a material mechanism without which the experience could not be supported. As indicated in chapter 2, the answers to these questions are not empty.

In terms of Chalmers' 'coherence' notions, the approach I advocate holds that the coherence between mechanism and experience is not just a 'brute fact' but does actually have a foundation in the informational link that Chalmers favours. This theory comes naturally and has been used in several parts of this book. Conscious beings have a natural affinity for such first person theories: even a child contemplating her joy at seeing an enticing piece of cake will realise that a stone cannot feel happy in the same way, but she will be able to recognise this inner state in a bee that is attracted by a pollen-laden flower. The point therefore is that we have a great predisposition for understanding which mechanisms are likely to contribute to consciousness and which are not.

In evoking five axioms I have simply done an outrageously rough introspective triage of phenomena which need different mechanisms to support them. Imagination is not the same as perception, emotion is not the same as imagination and so on. So in terms of Chalmers' 'coherence' discussions the axioms say that the coherence is not accidental but due to the material properties of specific mechanisms. At this point Chalmers' instinct that informational analysis is important becomes valid. The axiomatic experiences tie up with the informational properties of their mechanisms. Appendix 1 is intended to illustrate some of these informational links.

So here is a way of not being afraid of the 'hard' problem: start from the hard end of the relationship and work towards the 'easy' part.

Chapter 8

Unfinished Business

Detractors, Language, Deficits and Taboos

Looking back ...

This book could be summarised as advocating a robustly mechanistic approach to the understanding of consciousness. While many have advocated materialism, the seemingly strange step I have taken is to decompose what it is to be conscious into five individual components, the so-called axioms of this book. To recap, these features are: being a self in an out-there world, imagining such experiences whether fact or fiction, deploying attention which gives us access to vast amounts of information either in perception or imagination, being able to decide what to do next and the role that emotions play in all this. I argue that this gives us a taxing but manageable set of targets with which to unravel the way that the world gets into our minds and makes us say that we are conscious. Armed with these mechanisms, I also claim that much of what consciousness does in living beings including non-human animals can be explained and studied through virtual structures on a computer.

In Chapter 1 we saw that machines, in the sense of simulations on computers, can be useful in addressing and understanding these five mechanisms and the interactions between them. Complexity is the enemy of understanding, and the brain being the most complex machine on earth needs simulations and computer experimentation to clarify ideas. I am tired of people saying 'so you are looking at the brain but nobody knows how the brain works'. A tremendous amount is known of how the brain works. Neurology produces reams of results on a daily basis and the computer is a wonderful tool in piecing this together and beginning to see how the brain, as a complex system, actually works. Chapter 2 has made the link between the inwardly felt axioms and plausible brain mechanisms that could support them and could be tested on computers.

In the belief that the ideas necessary for explanations were well in place, I started to exercise these in chapter 3 with the attempt to explain what happens when we continue to be alive but are not conscious. It was seen that it is helpful to think of sleep as the 'resetting' of an intricate neural network. Then dreams are explained as the machinery of the first two axioms (perception and imagination) having to find a 'neutral' region in its collection of states. This causes the brain to revisit states formed during waking, conscious life but this occurs in incoherent sequences. Freud's unconscious then features as parts of the 'state structures' of all this experience, parts which have no access during waking life. In chapter 4 the axioms suggest that, to a large extent, animals are conscious as the higher species anyhow appear to possess the axiomatic mechanisms that we have. What are they doing there other than making the animal conscious?

Chapters 5 and 6 deal with the reality of consciousness in vision and the will respectively. Is that of which we are conscious an illusion or a reflection of reality? The axiomatic mechanisms favour the 'reflection of reality' interpretation with the odd illusionary effect being a slight malfunction of these systems. But, on the whole, the ultimate purpose of consciousness seems to be to internalise models of the world in as accurate a way as our sensory and axiomatic mechanisms allow. This enables us to plan our strategies before we go out there and start behaving.

However, a sceptic with a hardened view of the complexities of being conscious, may deploy a variety of arguments that severely question the above approach. In Chapter 7 I have addressed the criticisms by David Chalmers that an explanatory gap remains between easy (mechanistic) explanations and hard (first person) sensations. The upshot of this is that the existence of a gap seems to me to be harder to prove than the first axiom notion that all sensation has an identity with events occurring in brain mechanisms. Interestingly it is easy to agree with Chalmers that the route to a theory lies in informational rather than physical considerations. Indeed the mechanisms that underpin the axiomatic sensations are expressed in informational terms in this book.

But the hardened sceptic will not be deterred by a mere reference to the 'informational'. Raymond Tallis, for example, has led a tenacious and sustained attack not only against computer materialism but also against the suggestion that computer modelling of the brain has anything at all to offer. In the next section I shall describe Tallis' attacks and look at the way in which they can be defended.

Another criticism of the book so far could be that it left out completely the question of human language. There was a good reason for that: I tried to look at consciousness in a sufficiently general way so as to include living creatures outside of language-using humans. So here I shall spend a few paragraphs looking at the role of language in distinctly human forms of consciousness, before ending with a thought on what are taboos and what are real questions that still require an answer.

Tallis' Complaint

One of the most eloquent sceptics of computational and neurological approaches to consciousness is Raymond Tallis, a professor of geriatric medicine at Manchester University. He has written a summary of his many attacks published in books in a recent popular article[1] and a small book.[2] This is based on his own four axioms:

---

[1] Tallis, R. (2004), 'Why minds are not computers', *The Philosophers' Magazine,* issue 28, 4th Quarter, pp. 52–60.
[2] Tallis, R. (2004), *Why the Mind Is Not a Computer.* (Exeter: Imprint Academic).

- Computers are not conscious
- The conscious mind is not computational
- The centrality of consciousness to the mind cannot be denied
- Neuromythology is dangerous

Computers are not conscious

Of course not! Not even Tallis can point to computer modellers who maintain that the PCs and laptops that so dominate our lives are 'naturally' conscious. But there is a more subtle side to his complaint. He argues that *no* information processing system could be conscious in the sense of being aware of 'a world around them or being capable of happiness or despair'. Obviously this precludes anyone from referring to the brain as an 'information processing system'. But what does the brain do if not handle what is best called 'information'? Tallis directs his criticism at Chamers' suggestion (Chapter 7 in this book) that the analysis which is used to develop a theory of consciousness should be that of information systems. Tallis describes this suggestion as 'lunacy'. This is heart-felt stuff, but remains an opinion against Chalmers' logical argument: what drives the states of the brain is better addressed by concepts such as the state sequences, attractors and dynamics of informational systems than by the molecules and particles of chemistry and physics.

The trap that ensnares Tallis is to condemn *any* informational machine as evidently being incapable of being conscious because his laptop clearly is not. He fears that if we find one informational machine that is conscious, we will start granting consciousness to pocket calculators and telephone exchanges. Chalmers' (and, indeed, my own) argument is that only informational systems with a very specific structure might be conscious. Otherwise it's like believing that because bicycles can't fly, no heavier-than-air machine will fly. But given the right engine thrust and wing shape and, hey presto, you have 200 people winging their way across the sky. Given mechanisms that are capable of supporting the five axioms we have design principles for capturing consciousness in a machine without having to grant conciousness to my digital watch.

But Tallis has an objection to these 'specific mechanisms' too. For example, the feedback or re-entry that are crucial to mechanisms that support imagination and memory (Axiom 2) elicit from Tallis that it is 'laughably naïve' to believe that such internal connections 'will awaken such circuits to self-awareness'. But it is also laughably naïve to believe that the brain can sustain feelings of awareness *without* such feedback structures. The hippocampus is a sublime organ that coordinates the laying down of memories through being in a strategic position in several feedback loops. The same is true for very many other parts of the brain. Heeding Tallis' criticisms merely delays the understanding of what specific mechanisms are needed for an organism to be conscious. The history of science is full of such impediments: it was laughably naïve to think that the earth is not at the centre of the universe; it was laughably naïve to think that distant people could communicate through free space …

Consciousness is not computational.

The problem with understanding this phrase is the word 'computational'. Tallis takes the word at its surface value: computation is calculation. He then rightly points out that no number of repetitions of discrete circuits that do 2+2=4 can merge into that concrete whole that we feel when we are conscious. But looking just below the surface, computation is not calculation — it is a transformation of some kind. When the stones of Stonehenge filter a ray of light at sunrise onto a narrow target to signal the equinox, they are *computing* the position of the sun by transforming its ubiquitous light into an 'output' as a ray that shines on a stone. Similarly, computation in the context of being conscious is not calculation. Many computational events are involved in the brain: chemical transformations (as in neurotransmitter action), electrical transformations (as in neural firing), energy transformations (as in the retina: light to neural firing). In contrast with Tallis' narrow view of computation, it is precisely the language of information that analyses computational processes of the transformational kind as appears to underpin processes that make us conscious. This reveals natural, neural computations in brain structures , expressed as axioms here. This facilitates an ordered way of thinking about consciousness.

A neuron performs a very important computation: it makes a decision to fire or not to fire on the basis of the pattern of firing that impinges on it from other neurons. This produces prodigious firing patterns in vast fields of neurons all over the brain — we call these brain states. Whether it suits our philosophy or not, anything we feel is the result of some brain states, that is, the continuous and relentless computations that our neurons perform about 100 times a second. They work so fast and there are so many of them that they are credibly responsible for whatever it is that makes up our consciousness. Mostly, we are not conscious of the graininess of neural firing as it adds nothing to our proper interaction with the world. But we only need to shut our eyes and squeeze them a little to notice some snowy textures that show that neural firing can make itself felt under certain conditions. Or think of the way the pixels of a television screen that are replenished every 1/25th of a second without removing from our perception the impression of continuity. So to insist that consciousness is not computational is an obduracy at best based on too superficial a definition of computation, or possibly on a refusal to recognise that a man-made informational language is appropriate in discussions about consciousness.

To be fair, Tallis is aware of this type of discussion but counters it by saying that even given the most wonderful neural depiction, consciousness requires an *experiencer* of the neural dots to transform the dots into an experience. This is the well trodden fallacy of the infinite series if homunculi each of whom experiences the neural firing in the head of its predecessor. One can link consciousness to neural firing in at least two ways: one that requires an experiencer additional to the neural firing and one that accepts that the neural firing *is* the neural experiencer. The former becomes bogged down in the mire of infinite regress while the latter allows a theory such as the axiomatic one to survive. There is no compulsion, scientific or philosophical to embrace the first unhelpful assumption.

There is no mind without consciousness

At first, this seems to be a benign statement that does not impinge on computational approaches to consciousness. But the way Tallis deploys his argument is to point at AI functionalists who argue that 'mind' can be explained in terms of a heap of interacting mechanisms that are not conscious and that consciousness is merely something incidental to the system or a property inappropriately attributed by an observer who is impressed by the behaviour of the near zombie. Here I find a point of agreement. The thrust of depictive/axiomatic theory is that it does not run away from consciousness which is missing in computational/functional models such as those by Franklin as discussed in chapter 1. Indeed, it is difficult to define a mind without seeing that phenomenological consciousness is its main ingredient.

The dangers of neuromythology

It is here that Tallis launches a full frontal attack on my contention that what neurons do may usefully described as a rather specific computation. 'Indeed, much current neuroscience would be unthinkable without using terms from anthropomorphising computer talk.' It comes back to the word 'information' and Tallis points out that when this term is used for the transmission of conscious ideas among people it is one thing, but when it is used in computers it is merely a measure of the capacity of a cable to transfer pulses that have no meaning until interpreted by a human being.

Of course, the latter was the case for information as defined by the 'statistical theory of information' brilliantly derived by Claude Shannon in the 1950s (see Aleksander, 2003).[3] Shannon defined the 'bit' as the amount of information contained in a device or signal that can be in one of two states (on/off, 0/1, True/False, smokepuff/nosmokepuff). Indeed, Shannon was not concerned with the meaning of signals. It is also true that much of what is called information as processed by information

---

[3]   Aleksander, I. (2003), 'Information bit by bit'. In *It Must Be Beautiful*, ed. Graham Farmelo (London: Granta).

processing machinery does not concern itself with meaning. This is not because signals cannot represent meaning for users of the processing machinery, but because it is less usual to think in terms of information which is *meaningful to the machine*.

So is there something that could be said to have meaning for a machine and through this validate machine models of consciousness? Indeed this is precisely what this book has been about. Depiction in axioms 1 and 3 is meaningful *to the machine* as it positions the self (point of view) of the machine in an out-there world. Axiom 2 (imagination) relates perception to earlier experience which is meaningful because it guides the behaviour of the machine (axiom 4) according to an evaluation of the emotional reactions to perception. There is no need for a human to get into the loop — 5-axiom machines are autonomous. The depictive firing patterns of their mechanisms contain the meaning of the world and the machine's place in it. This is sufficiently close to any definition of meaning in neurology.

In summary, yes, laptops are not conscious, but consciousness *is* computational in the very broad sense that every element whether a cell, a group of cells an architecture of a group of cells or the organism interacting with its world can be expressed in the language of informational systems as opposed to the language of physics or chemistry. There is no neuromythology — informationally analysed 5-axiom systems have a neurology which parallels and helps us to understand the living variety.

Language: Wittgenstein's undoubted influence

What might be the implications of the axiomatic/depictive outlook on being conscious for language? Clearly, as I introspect about my consciousness, language looms large. Later I shall ask whether this requires a new axiom, while, in the meantime, I need to acknowledge the enormous influence that Ludwig Wittgenstein has had on philosophical discussion of the nature of language. Well-known is the fact that there were two contributions to this, the first from *Tractatus Logico Philosophicus*[4] and a contrasting one from the later *Philosophical Investigations*.[5]

The earlier contribution was concerned with the way that language conveys factual information about what is in the world. It endowed words with meaning without being too concerned with the origin of the word in the speaker's mind or the effect that the word might have on the mind of the listener. Wittgenstein imagined that there was some pictorial representation of a word in mind, but one that has a complex and unexplained relationship to language. So 'time flies like an arrow' and 'fruit flies like sugar' could be distinguished because their pictorial qualities are different. In the axiomatic ideas of this book, what this says is that the action of axiom 2 machinery cannot be fooled by a seeming similarity between those two sentences. This seems to support Wittgenstein's early ideas but puts a great onus on the way in which axiom 2 machinery retrieves its depictions. This problem is currently being researched in my laboratory. However, an early result of axiomatic thinking shows one departure from Wittgenstein's line of thought. He suggested that language represented everything in the world that could be said and, therefore, restricted everything that could be thought. In contrast, the mechanisms visited in this book suggest that everything that can be thought is limited by the depictive apparatus of the brain. This is why we have such difficulty in grasping notions of quantum theory if we are not used to thinking in abstract terms. Nothing like 'entanglement' (influence of a particle on another that is not linked to it in any way) can ever be experienced, it has to be believed and then checked for mathematical consistency. Language then evolves to express what can be thought. This is why, because we (or, to be precise, a very restricted number of people) want to think of abstract features of the physical world we have invented the language of mathematics.

[4]   Wittgenstein, L. (1922), *Tractatus Logico- Philosophicus*, English translation by D.F. Pears and B.F. McGuinness (London: Routledge and Kegan Paul).
[5]   Wittgenstein, L. (1953) *Philosophical Investigations*, English translation by G.E.M. Anscombe (Oxford: Blackwell).

But back with Wittgenstein's later ideas, he placed language in the role of an integral part of human existence, hence part of the human mind. While in the earlier ideas his focus was much on factual statements (e.g. 'birds are known to fly') as opposed to abstract expressions (e.g. 'I believe that the Earth is flat'), in later thoughts he attempted to include all that language is used for, including non-factual utterances. This brought into play the need to have common meaning between speakers to preserve communication. It suggests that whatever notion the speaker has in mind, he can select an utterance to create, in the listener's mind, a representation of whatever part of his mental state the speaker intends to communicate. I have no doubt that Wittgenstein's broader view of language is correct. It is now proper to ask how axiomatic models might address both factual and abstract transmission.

An axiomatic language philosophy

Axioms are due to phenomena that appear to be important in an introspective trawl of what it is to be conscious. There is no doubt that my ability to use language is an important part of my consciousness. Is there a case for language being a 'sixth axiom'? In arguing that there is, I bear in mind that it is largely a human competence where consciousness, as I have suggested in these pages, cannot be dismissed in non-human animals. So language is not necessary for consciousness, but an elaborative evolution of the apparatus that produces consciousness in the entire animal kingdom may be responsible for language in humans.

So axiom 6 might read 'I can selectively communicate that of which I am conscious to others'. Why should that be useful? Michael Arbib[6] of the University of Southern California argues that consciousness and language have co-evolved in humans for the primary purpose of coordinating the members of a social group. The group is best organised if individuals communicate to others what they plan to do next (albeit selectively — individuals can lie). This requires the creation of outward signs that

---

[6]   Arbib, M. (2001), 'Co-evolution of human consciousness and language', *Annals of the New York Academy of Sciences*, **929**.

selectively represent the internal depictions involved in planning and its emotional evaluation. The implication of this is that the complexity of language depends on the complexity of what can be depicted in the awareness areas of the system (see the familiar fig A7 in the appendix). But it is more than this. Consider the difference between the two statements:

(a) I am seeing Jane smiling at me.

(b) I am thinking of Jane smiling at me.

The depiction in awareness areas for the above two expressions is likely to be similar. However, the linguistic expression includes not only the informational state of what is depicted, but a decoding of where in the system the depiction leading to awareness is taking place. Sentence (a) refers to activity in the perceptual module while (b) is largely in the imagination module. Of course this is the same mechanism which is at work when perceived events are distinguished from imagined ones. Despite the overlap of the content of imaginary and perceptual areas in sensation which is due to depictive referencing, the sensation of seeing and imagining is distinguished by where and how it occurs. So if the predominant sensation is in the imagination module the system has no difficulty into decoding this as something like 'I am thinking' or if the sensation is formed in the perceptual area, this would be decoded as 'I am seeing'.

It would be tempting at this point merely to invent a new neural box to be added to fig. A7: a box that decodes overall states of the system into language and receives language to provide state adjustments to the existing modules. But this would be unwise for two main reasons. First, while there is some localisation and specialisation for language in living brains, the dependence of proper functioning of language can be discovered in many areas of the brain[7] and not in one prominent outgrowth. Second, such an area would imply a much larger difference in brain architecture between language-using and non-language animals.

---

[7] Caplan, D.N. (2005), 'Language: Neuropsychology'. In (Gregory, ed.) *The Oxford Companion of the Mind, 2nd ed.* (Oxford University Press).

So the challenge for discovering the machine implications of axiom 6 is to do this within the framework of figure A7. Although this is still a structure that will be researched for some time to come, an introspective approach within this framework may be developed. I suggest an approach in which one treats language production mechanisms as being closely linked to the volitional mechanisms discussed in Chapter 6. That is, utterances are formulated in the Imagination Module and follow the same process of decision making as do plans in general. The following scenario might be useful:

> I recently heard that a distant friend, Mary, had a car accident in which her husband was killed while she was unhurt. I see her coming towards me in the street. I begin to think of what I might say.

Here are three possible utterances:

(a) I heard about John — I'm terribly sorry.

(b) Hello Mary, how are you?

(c) Mary! You must be devastated, what can I do to help?

These utterances have distinct emotional connotations, that would also be depicted in the imagination module according to arguments on volition (Chapter 6).

Utterance (a) projects a direct informational statement and an indication of a 'self' that is distressed; (b) is dishonest as it hides knowledge of the death of John; (c) projects a helpful 'self'. The evaluations in the emotion module might be neutral for (a), negative for (b) due to its lack of honesty and positive for (c) due to its altruism. So according to the principles of Chapter 6 it would be (c) that triggers the action module, this time to generate speech related to the (c) mental state. The key point is that this view of uttering requires no new mechanisms over and above volitional ones. However, a salient question that remains to be answered is how grammar on the one hand and meaning on the other get involved in these mechanisms.

It is here that the influence of Noam Chomsky, MIT linguistics professor and a political 'conscience' in the US become important.

Axioms and Chomsky's theory of language

In a disarmingly clear review of his own contribution to the theory of language, Noam Chomsky[8] asks and answers three major questions:

(i)   What do we know when we are said to know a language?

(ii) What is the basis for the growth of this knowledge?

(iii) How is this knowledge put in use?

The answers clearly encompass Chomsky's highly influential contribution to contemporary linguistics.

(i)   We know a system of rules, a grammar, that generates an infinite set of 'correct' expressions which, due to adherence to the grammatical rules convey meaning.

(ii) The fundamental properties of these rules are part of the innate endowment of a developing person.

(iii) To utter an idea present in mind the person employs a 'performance model' that accesses the innate grammatical endowment.

The main source of difficulty that feeds arguments of Chomsky's detractors is the 'innate endowment' of grammatical rules. I have written elsewhere of the acrimonious debate between Chomsky and the Swiss psychologist Jean Piaget who decried the 'endowment' idea and argued that 'development' could achieve the same ends.[9] A more recent alternative to endowment was first expressed by Richard Dawkins[10] and then elaborated by Susan Blackmore:[11] ideas (or memes) as held by human societies have a character that coevolves with the evolution of societies and their expression in language has this evolutionary character too (in line with Arbib's thought expressed earlier). In other words the repository of grammar and usage is society itself rather than the individual. A developing child in this society picks up this usage as the best way to express his

[8]   Chomsky, N. (2005), Language: Chomsky's Theory. In (Gregory, ed.) *The Oxford Companion of the Mind, 2nd ed.*(Oxford University Press).

[9]   Aleksander, I. (1996), *Impossible Minds, My Neurons, My Consciousness.* (London, Imperial College Press).

[10] Dawkins, R. (1976), *The Selfish Gene* (Oxford University Press).

[11] Blackmore, S.J. (1999), *The Meme Machine* (Oxford University Press).

ideas to his peers. Examples of children brought up by wild animals support this notion as they sometimes never acquire a full ability to master language.

The axiomatic approach leans more heavily towards memetic rather than genetic evolution. Without going into detail, the axiomatic answers to Chomsky's three questions take the following form.

(i)   To know a language is to have linguistic muscular action tied closely to the state structures of the imagination module.

(ii) This grows as the depictive state structure in the imagination module grows: through the interaction of the organism with objects in the world and the expression of language from other individuals.

(iii) With this structure, thought and language become indivisible, the decision regarding which thoughts we choose to articulate being driven by the interplay between emotion, imaginative planning and action as for any other decision to act.

In summary, language and actions in the world go hand in hand in the sense that language like actions is planned, emotionally assessed and uttered as a result of this assessment. Like learning to use a short knife in the action of opening oysters, one learns language tools by discovering how others use them. Grammar arises as a standardising force sustained by society and learned by individuals not as rules but usage. Grammar as learned at school is a confirming activity that legitimises usage. We may have a feeling for what happens if we fill our bag several times with four marbles at a time, but learning multiplication tables makes this knowledge explicit and secure. We are not genetically endowed with multiplication tables.

When things go wrong ....

It is one of the ironies of life that those who escape the ravages of major physical illnesses such as cancer or heart failure, become open to attack by deficits of the brain. Alzheimer's disease, various dementias and Parkinson's disease are afflictions that bring misery and suffering to the end of the lives of far too many. Of course research in neurology laboratories is intense, but progress is slow due to the immense complexity of the brain. I have maintained that, starting with what the sufferer feels, it may be possible to trace this to a failure in depictive mechanisms and in this way gain a better understanding of the deficit and how to care for sufferers.

With Helen Morton of Brunel University I worked on a specific project that involves Parkinson's disease sufferers.[12] It was discovered by Chis Kennard and his colleagues in the neuroscience department of Imperial College that some Parkinson's sufferers had difficulties in solving visual problems that involve rearranging a set of 3 coloured spheres in 3 slots[13]. The participants were shown the current state of the balls and a target state and asked to work out a set of moves that would rearrange the balls so as to achieve the target state. The experimenters tracked eye movements and discovered that while normally the eyes would range purposively between the current state of the balls and the target, some Parkinson's sufferers would shift their gaze from the one to the other in an arbitrary fashion without being able to solve the puzzle. But not being able to solve visual puzzles would not be such dreadful thing, it is the suspicion that this visual deficit leads to seeming confusion among sufferers in planning daily tasks such as making a cup of tea or recognising the face of someone they know.

Normally Parkinson's sufferers have their ability to control movement disrupted by a lack of the neurotransmitter dopamine in those parts of the brain that control movement. This leads to characteristic tremors, inability to walk and fixed face expressions that are usually associated with the disease. The question that looms over these results is whether the poor performers are beginning to suffer from some additional cognitive deficits, or dementias which were weakening their planning abilities, or whether the visual deficit is just part of the muscular effect of dopamine shortages.

---

[12] Aleksander, I. and Morton, H. (2003), 'A digital neural model of visual deficits in Parkinson's disease', *Proc. IWANN 03* (Heidelberg: Springer).

[13] Hodgson TL, Bajwa A, Owen AM, Kennard C. (2000), 'The strategic control of gaze direction in the Tower-of-London task', *Cognitive Neuroscience*, **12** (5), 894–907.

Using axiomatic ideas we set out to see whether the latter hypothesis could be sustained: in what sense could a muscular problem cause a visual planning deficit? The key organ in the brain that controls eye movement is the *superior colliculus* (SC) which has its own map of the visual field. It unconsciously moves the foveal eye gaze to areas in that field where things are changing in space or time. So the eye 'saccades' to contrasts in the visual field and things that move. But it does much more than that: the SC may move the eyes to areas that help to recognise an object such as a face through receiving signals from the perceptual reconstruction areas of the brain or even to move in the direction of a perceived sound, being alerted by the auditory parts of the brain.

However, wherever the SC receives its driving signals from, it has the task of positioning the eye with a great deal of precision for the consciousness-creating reconstruction to work according to axiom 1. This accuracy is achieved by the SC being in a control loop that rapidly removes the error between the target fixation position and the actual position. To solve a visual puzzle, the SC receives its fixation targets from higher brain areas that develop a solution strategy. However, it is also known that the SC receives input from the basal ganglia, which are dopamine generating areas of the brain. This begins to support the hypothesis that a lack of dopamine might disrupt low level vision processing by affecting the SC. The dopamine input to the SC acts as a stabilising agent that ensures the accuracy of fixation finding. Remove it and the loop will become inaccurate. We devised a way of measuring the low level visual action directly, and predicted the result of a possible instability due to low dopamine generation. Cognitive dementias could then be distinguished from mechanical deficits of the visual fixation loop: the latter, in terms of time and accuracy of remembering seen shapes on a screen would have different time/accuracy characteristics from cognitive errors.

It turned out that the low-level hypothesis was supported. However, the above was a feasibility study that suggested that much more work of this kind could and should be done. Paradoxically, the implication of the understanding that can arise through using machine analyses is that people may be treated *less* as if they were machines. That is if a sufferer whose low level machinery is faulty gets lumped together with those less fortunate who have real cognitive deficits, this would be sad: a bit like saying that someone with gout cannot be distinguished from someone with a gangrenous leg because they both have painful legs.

There is enormous scope for further work for machine modelling of other mental deficits. For example, the afflictions of schizophrenics as an undue dominance of imaginative depiction over the perceptual kind and the emotional confusion that this can cause. This would benefit not only the elderly as schizophrenia is most often present in the young.

Fighting taboos

Some have suggested that those interested in machine consciousness are merely venting their iconoclastic desires against the attitudes on mind soul and consciousness provided by a variety of religions. It is the word 'attitude' that is key in the above sentence. Any form of science could be said to replace attitudes with formalisms. Galileo replaced the attitudes of the theologian savants of the sixteenth century with hard fought-for models of the universe based on observation and logic. I do not feel that science and religions are in long term conflict. Short term, yes: there was no restraint in the persecution of the likes of Galileo and others who questioned a contemporary theological belief. But the dynamic between science and religion seems to me to be simple. Science is that which has been made rational by theory and experiment, but science is incomplete at any point in time: the unknown merely shifts to new areas. What remains might need to have a place in people's minds even if science does not address it. Religion as a logical object plays the role of a set of unproven hypotheses that are necessary for individuals to behave in a stable way so as to sustain communities. It was convenient for Galileo's accusers to believe in the universal immobility and centrality of the earth in heaven, explaining its favoured position in the eyes of God. This gave God and his representatives on earth the authority to determine what is a proper (that is, stable) way of life. So Galileo and his telescope were a threat.

But the pressure on the border between science and religion comes from the science side. Galileo and his successor soul-mates get their way in the end if their science is sound and eventually appeals to intelligent theologians who then continue to provide support for stable life in different fields.

And so it is with models of mind and consciousness. In chapter 7, I exposed a whiff of the important influence that religious philosophers had on our culture in telling plausible stories that explain volition with very close implications for leading good or evil lives. Will machine consciousness destroy the notion of 'being *good* to please God who is always watching those he has made in his own *good* image'? There is no rational reason for this outlook if an alternative can be found in science. A proper understanding of the mechanisms of volition and other aspects of being conscious simply removes from theology the need to create explanations based in divinity. This is like it no longer being necessary to evoke the almighty in an explanation of the creation of life on earth: the theory of evolution replaces the seven days of creation for most of us. The latter becomes a metaphor that may no longer be necessary. It may be better to understand good and evil as stabilising and destabilising forces within our panoply of imaginative states in axiom 2, rather than to pander to a belief in mystical divine links. After all we do not drive with due care and attention only to please police officers, we recognise the proven dangers.

There is therefore nothing blasphemous about conscious machines, but the concept is relatively new and might shock the believer. I hope that this book has shown ways for lifting some of the taboos that guide the image we have of ourselves, of being conscious, of having imagination, of being in control of our relationships of regarding other life forms and of creating novel forms of machinery which might naturally regard their mechanistic selves as being conscious. There is a vast amount of work to be done to have a comfortable syntactic science of being conscious. I hope that bright young minds will be attracted to this exciting road into the future.

Appendix

Technicalities of Brain-Like Automata

A1. The Class of Brain-like Machines

Throughout this book reference is made to the relationship of mind to body being similar to informational states of a machine and the function of its parts. The type of informational machine to which this refers is not a computer. While a computer certainly processes information it is entirely set up to execute the instructions of a program. This creates a vast gap between the way that the brain processes information and the way that a computer does it. So, here I define and give examples of the operation of a specific class of informational machine whose very definition includes the brain.

1. The machine is cellular.

2. The function of cells can be adaptable.

3. Cells exist in modules where they are connected to one another as well as having some of their connections influenced from outside the module. All or some of the cell outputs are available to feed other modules.

4. The machine is made up of many modules.

5. The machine has inputs from outside (sensory) and produces output actions.

6. The function of the machines is described by referring to nested collections of states that exist inside the machine at any point in time and over time: cell states, module states and machine states.

The first five items above describe the 'body' of the machine and the sixth one its 'mind'. The information processes are studied in terms of the fact the states in 6 vary with time providing a 'contemplative' link between sensory inputs and actions.

A2. A particular digital brain-like machine

So far this has been a very general description that includes the way that the brain processes information. In what follows, functions will be assigned to cells etc. that are much simpler than those found in the brain, but without losing the *style* in which the brain might process information. In this way I can attempt to support some of the arguments found in the body of this book.

The cell

The basic cell bears a similarity to the neurons in the brain in the sense that it maps patterns at its inputs into decisions at its outputs.

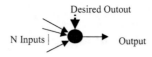

Figure A1: Symbol for a cell

The cell has the following important connections.

Output (O):
0 (not firing), 1 (firing), D (don't know — fires or not fires in a random sequence)

Input (I):
Receives inputs from the outputs of other cells. There are N inputs.

Desired Output (DO):
Receives 0 or 1 to force the output to that value and associate that value with the N-input pattern present at the time. It can also be switched off so as not to affect the cell. This is the means whereby the cell learns.

It has *a local memory* which remembers the response to the N-point input patterns. This works as follows. To start with all the input patterns are associated with the output D Every time the DO terminal is activated by the value 0 or 1, that value becomes associated in perpetuity with the current input. This is the process of *training*. If the stored desired output for a particular input is contradicted by DO, then the associated symbol returns to D and the cell responds with arbitrary 0s or 1s to that input. Where the DO receives its input from is part of the system structure and will differ depending on what the structure requires.

Response strategy.

How does a cell respond to an input pattern it has not been trained on? It is known that neurons in the brain 'generalise', that is they respond to unknown patterns in the same way as they would for a similar, but trained pattern.

In the simplified cell, given an unknown pattern P_u, and given a set of trained patterns P_1, P_2, P_3 ... with corresponding responses R_1, R_2, R_3 ... the best match is found among the training patterns (say P_x) and its trained response (R_x) generated. This is described as finding the 'nearest neighbour' of P_x.

Of course a straight match may not be found and the unknown pattern may match several trained patterns with differing responses. In this case the out put D (random sequence of 0s and 1s)

Example: Say that the cell has six inputs (N=6) and the training patterns are:

```
000000 responds with 0
111111 responds with 1
100011 responds with 0
110001 responds with 1
```

Say that the unknown input is 000001, then

it matches the first pattern in 5 positions
it matches the second pattern in 1 position
it matches the third pattern in 4 positions
it matches the fourth pattern in 4 positions.

There is a clear best match and the cell will respond with a 0.

However, pattern 101100 has matches, 3, 3, 2 and 2 respectively, hence there is no clear match and the cell will respond with a random sequence, (something like 01001101011000 …)

Generalisation control

In the brain it is most likely that neurons do not always generalise by the same amount: sometime they respond only if the pattern is very close to the training patterns while at other times they may be more tolerant. (Anaesthesia in Chapter 3 is an example of this).

I can incorporate this into the above cell model. It is possible to specify a 'generalisation radius' G as the fraction of inputs that has to match the unknown pattern before any decision other than D is made. So, in the above example, if G is set to 2/3, any pattern that at best matches the trained patterns in less than four positions is given the output D. Clearly setting G to 1 will cause the cell to respond only to the training patterns.

Modules

A module is a group of cells that act cooperatively to produce an overall effect. The prototypical arrangements are shown in figure A2: on the left is a regular net and on the right this is redrawn as an array of cells. What distinguishes a module is the

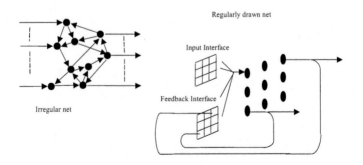

Figure A2: A neural module, drawn irregularly (left) or as a regular array (right).

fact that cells receive inputs from the outputs of other cells (feedback) within the module. Some cells receive inputs from outside of the module. The output of all the cells taken together form the *state* of the module. This could be different from the *output* of the module which is a sampling of the state (i.e. only some cell outputs project outside the module).

The only difference between the irregular net on the left and its regular re-drawing on the right is that the latter allows one to track the processing of two-dimensional patterns that might be depictions of out-there 2-D worlds (see Chapter 2).

Memory and attractors in modules

It is possible to demonstrate the effect of feedback as follows. First consider a 3x3 net as at the right of figure A2. Imagine that every cell receives inputs from its corresponding point on the input interface. So here there is no feedback. Some of the connections are shown in fig. A3 below together with some of the patterns to be processed.

Say that the task of the of the net is to depict the two patterns also shown in fig. 3 (call them + and X. That is, when one of the patterns is present at the input, its equivalent should be formed as a state of the array. This is done by placing + or X on the input interface and forcing the cells to fire with the same pattern using the DO inputs (not shown for clarity).

Each cell has therefore learned to associate a sample of the input pattern with its desired output. Clearly if the + and X patterns are presented at the input, they will be reproduced in the state array. However, the module just becomes a transmitter of any input pattern. The selectivity of the module depends on the

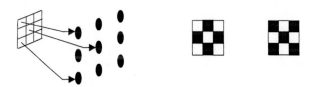

Figure A3: Some of the input connections for example 2 and patterns to be processed (Black = firing or 1, white= not firing or 0).

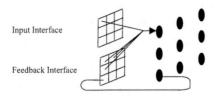

Input Interface

Feedback Interface

Figure A4: Each cell now receives inputs not only from the corresponding point in the input matrix, but also from their own output and the output of neighbouring cells (from the right and from below — the matrix is imagined as being wrapped around the sides and top to bottom) .

number of points on the input interface that each cell is connected. Clearly if each cell were to be connected to *all* the interface inputs, **+** and the X would be depicted for these two patterns and those similar to them.

To understand the effect of feedback, we bring the feedback interface into play as shown in fig. A4.

The module is trained to depict again by forcing the required pattern on the cells with the same pattern present at the input interface. The feedback interface therefore also receives this pattern. For practical reasons it is assumed that the feedback interface holds the previous state while the new state is being computed and is then updated at the arrival of a regularly produced timing pulse.

What happens can be predicted very laboriously using pencil and paper. It's better to either write a program or use an available simulation (I used NRM … see…).[1] Take, for example, the top left cell. Fig. A5. shows what the top left cell has learned. The

Figure A5: Showing what the top left cell has learned due to training on the two basic patterns. Taking the cell inputs clockwise from the East position, it has learned to output 0 for an input of 0110 and 1 for an input of 1001.

[1] Aleksander, I., Dunmall, B. & Del Frate, V. (1999), 'Neurocomputational models of visualisation', *Proc. IWANN 99* (Heidelberg: Springer).

same can be done for all the other cells. Then, given any input pattern and state pattern, the next state pattern can be predicted.

This allows us to understand why it is said that the module with feedback has memory. Let both the input pattern and the state pattern be all-0. The top left cell has an input of 0000 using the convention in the figure. This is equally 'distant' from both the inputs learned by this cell, meaning that the cell is in the D state and will next output a 0 or a 1 arbitrarily. The same is true for all the other cells. So the next state will be totally arbitrary. However, say that with an all-0 state pattern the input is all-0 except for the top left cell. Now the input to that cell is 0001 which is closer to the learned 1001 than 0110, so that cell will output a 1. Then the nearby cells too will have inputs that are closer to the X pattern than the **+** one and will respond to make the second state more like the X. the rest of the cells still output arbitrarily. But the next time around the X will 'spread' to the other cells ending in a stable X even if the input is all-0. The module has

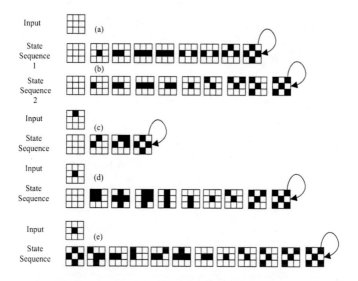

Figure A6: Examples of state sequences. (a) and (b) show that, starting with all-0, the system can finish in either of the learned patterns. (c) and (d) show that with a fragment of a learned state at the input, the correct pattern is found. (e) is an example of how one learned stable pattern can be changed into the other by a fragment of the appropriate input.

Appendix

'remembered' the X pattern. Some of these sequences are shown in fig. A6.

Fig A6 also allows me to explain in what sense the module can be said to have 'attractors' as follows. The module has a 'state space' that is made up of all the possible output states of the nine cells, that is 512 (that is, 2^9) patterns or states. Starting in one such state and given an input, the resulting sequence is a path traced out in the state space. Of course, because some cells for a particular state can be in the D state, there is an equal probability of several states being next. We have seen this in the very first step of sequences (a) and (b). However, whatever the path chosen with the all zero input, the system always ends in one of the two trained patterns. It is in this sense that these states are said to be *attractors* of the state of the system. Once an attractor has been reached, the state stops changing. In the case of (d) and (e) there

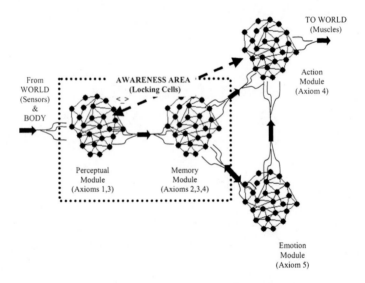

Figure A7: A minimal architecture with axiomatic/depictive properties. The perceptual module directly depicts sensory input and can be influenced by bodily input such as pain and hunger. The memory module implements non-perceptual thought for planning and recall of experience. The memory and perceptual modules overlap in awareness as they are both locked to either current or remembered world events The emotion module evaluates the 'thoughts' in the memory module and the action module causes the best plan to reach the actions of the organism.

is only one attractor in the net — the appropriate remembered depictive state.

A3. A digital implementation of a depictive system.

The scheme described in fig. A7 is a minimal architecture that shows how a digital neural architecture can accommodate the five axioms of chapter 2.

The content of figure A7 is the physical structure necessary for a minimal implementation of the five axioms. This is taken further in several parts of this book.

Bibliography

Aleksander, I. (1996), *Impossible Minds, My Neurons, My Consciousness* (London, Imperial College Press).

Aleksander, I. (2000), *How to build a Mind: Dreams and Diaries* (London: Weidenfeld and Nicolson; paperback ed. Phoenix 2001).

Aleksander, I. (2003), 'Information bit by bit'. In *It must be beautiful* Ed. Graham Farmelo (London: Granta).

Aleksander, I. and Dunmall, B. (2003), 'Axioms and tests for the presence of minimal consciousness in agents', *Journal of Consciousness Studies,***10** (4-5), 7-19.

Aleksander, I., Dunmall, B. and Del Frate, V. (1999), 'Neurocomputational models of visualisation', *Proc. IWANN 99* (Heidelberg: Springer).

Aleksander, I. and Morton, H. (2003), 'A digital neural model of visual deficits in Parkinson's disease', *Proc. IWANN 03* (Heidelberg: Springer).

Aleksander, I. and Morton, H.B. (1995), *An Introduction to Neural Computing* (London: International Thompson Computer Press).

Aleksander, I. Dunmall, B. (2000), 'An extension to the hypothesis of the asynchrony of visual consciousness', *Proc Royal Soc. London, B,* **267** (1439), 197–200.

Arbib, M. (2001), 'Co-evolution of human consciousness and language', *Annals of the New York Academy of Sciences,* **929**.

Aserinsky, E and Kleitman, N. (1953), 'Regular periods of eye motility and concomitant phenomena during sleep', *Science,***118**, 273.

Baars, B.J. (1997), *In the Theater of Consioucness* (New York: Oxford University Press).

Blackmore, S.J. (1999), *The Meme Machine* (Oxford University Press).

Bootzin, R.R., Khilstrom, J.F. and Schachter, D.L., ed. (1990), *Sleep and Cognition* (Washington: APA).

Breger, L. (1969), 'Dream function: An information processing model', In L. Breger (Ed.), *Clinical-Cognitive Psychology* (New Jersey: Prentice-Hall).

Caplan, D.N. (2005), 'Language: Neuropsychology', In (Gregory, Ed) *The Oxford Companion of the Mind (2nd edition).*(Oxford University Press)

Carruthers, P. (2000), *Phenomenal Consciousness: A Naturalist Theory* (Cambridge University Press).

Cartwright, R.D. (1978), *A Primer on Sleep and Dreaming* (London: Addison Wesley).

Cartwright, R.D. (1990), 'A network model of dreams'. In Bootzin et al. (ed.), *Sleep and Cognition*, chapter 13.

Cartwright, R. and Ratzel, R. (1972), 'Effects of dream loss on waking behaviors', *Archives of General Psychiatry*, **27**, 277–280.

Chalmers, D.J. (1996), *The Conscious Mind: In Search of a Fundamental Theory* (New York: Oxford University Press).

Chomsky, N. (2005), 'Language: Chomsky's Theory'. In (Gregory, Ed) *The Oxford Companion of the Mind (2nd edition)*.(Oxford: Oxford University Press).

Crick, F. and Koch, C. (1998), 'Consciousness and neuroscience', *Cereb Cortex*, **8** (2), 97–107.

Crick, F. and Koch, C. (2003), 'A framework for consciousness', *Nature Neuroscience*, **6**, 119–126.

Crick, F. and Mitchison, G. (1983), 'The function of dream and sleep', *Nature*, **304**, 111–114.

Crick, F. and Mitchison, G. (1986), 'REM sleep and neural nets', *Journal of Mind and Behaviour*,**7**, 229–250.

Crick, F.H.C.(1994), *The Astonishing Hypothesis* (London: Simon and Schuster).

Davies, H. and Bradford, S.A. (1987), 'Counting behaviour in rats in a simulated natural environment', *Ethology*, **73**, 265–80.

Dawkins, R. (1976), *The Selfish Gene* (Oxford University Press).

Dement, W. (1960), 'The effect of dream deprivation', *Science*, **131**, 1705–1707.

Dennett, D.C. (1991), *Consiousness Explained* (London: Allen Lane).

Edelman, G. and Tononi, G. (2000), *A Universe of Consciousness: How Matter Becomes Imagination* (New York: Basic Books).

Franklin, S. (2003), 'IDA, a conscious artefact?', *Journal of Consciousness Studies*, **10** (4–5), 47–66.

Freud, S. (1955), *The Interpretation of Dreams* (New York: Basic Books).

Galletti, C. and Battaglini, P. (1989), 'Gaze-Dependent Visual Neurons in Area V3A of Monkey prestriate cortex', *J. Neurosci*, **9**, 1112–1125.

Griffin, D. (1992), *Animal Minds* (University of Chicago Press).

Hamlyn, D.W. (1990), *The Penguin History of Western Philosophy* (London: Penguin Books).

Harrington, D.L. and Haaland, K.Y. (1999), 'Neural underpinnings of temporal processing: A review of focal lesion, pharmacological and functional imaging research', *Rev. Neurosci.*, **10** (2), 91–116.

Hebb, D.O. (1949), *The Organisation of Behaviour* (New York: Chapman and Hall).

Hobson, J.A. and McCarley, R.W. (1977), 'The brain as a dream generator: An activation-synthesis hypothesis of the dream process', *American Journal of Psychiatry*, **134**, 1335-1348.

Hodgson, T.L., Bajwa, A., Owen, A.M. and Kennard C. (2000), 'The strategic control of gaze direction in the Tower-of-London task', *Cognitive Neuroscience*. **12**, 5, 894-907.

Holland, O. ed. (2003), *Machine Consciousness* (Exeter: Imprint Academic).

Jackson, F. (1982), 'Epiphenomenal qualia', *Philosophical Quarterly*, **32**, 127–36

James, W. (1904), 'Does consciousness exist?', *Journal of Philosophy, Psychology and Scientific Methods*, **1**, 477–491.

James, W., (1890), *The Principles of Psychology* (London: MacMillan).

Koch, C , Crick, F. (2001), 'The zombie within', *Nature*, **411**, 893.

Ladd, G. (1982), 'Contributions to the psychology of visual dreams', *Mind*, **1**, 299–304.

Libet, B., Wright, E.W., and Pearl, D.K. (1983), 'Time of conscious intention to act in relation to onset of cerebral activity (readiness potential): The unconscious initiation of a free voluntary act', *Brain*, **106**, 623–42.

Marr, D. (1982), *Vision: A Computational Investigation into the Human Representation and Processing of Visual Information* (San Francisco: Freeman).

Nagel, T. (1974), 'What's it like to be a bat?', *Philosophical Review*, **83**, 435–50.

Noë, A. and O'Regan, J. K. (2000), 'Perception, Attention and the Grand Illusion', *Psyche*, **6** (15).

Noë, A., ed. (2002), *Is the Visual World a Grand Illusion?* (Exeter: Imprint Academic).

O'Regan, J.K. and Noë, A. (2001), 'A sensorimotor account of vision and visual consciousness', *Behavioural and Brain Sciences*, **24** (5).

Rilling, M.E. and Neiworth, J.J. (1991), 'How animals use images', *Sci Prog.*, **75** (298 Pt 3-4), 439–52.

Roffwarg,, H., Muzio, J. and Dement, W. (1966), 'Ontogenic development of the human sleep-dream cycle', *Science*, **152**, 604–619.

Rosenthal, D. (1993), 'Thinking that one thinks'. In M. Davies and G. Humphreys (eds.) *Consciousness*, 197–223 (Oxford: Blackwell).

Rosenthal, D. (2002), 'The HOT model of consciousness', In Rita Carter, *Consciousness* (London: Weidenfeld and Nicholson).

Shear, J., ed. (1995), *Explaining Consciousness: The Hard Problem* (Cambridge, MA: MIT Press).

Sherry, D.F. (1984), 'Food storage, memory and marsh tits',. *Animal Behaviour*, **32**, 451–64.

Simons, D.J. and Chabris. C.F. (1999), 'Gorillas in our midst: sustained inattentional blindness for dynamic events', *Perception*, **28** (9), 1059–1074.

Snyder, F. (1966), 'Towards an evolutionary theory of dreaming', *American Journal of Psychiatry*, **123**, 121–136.

Stamp Dawkins, M. (1998), *Through Our Eyes Only: The Search for Animal Consciousness* (Oxford University Press).

Tallis, R. (2004), 'Why minds are not computers', *The Philosophers' Magazine*, **28** (4), 52–60.

Tallis, R. (2004), *Why the Mind is not a Computer* (Exeter: Imprint Academic).

Terrace, H.S. (1991), 'Chunking during serial learning by a pigeon: I. Basic evidence', *J Exp Psychol Anim Behav Process.*, **17** (1), 81–93.

von Frisch K.(1967), *The Dance Language and Orientation of Bees* (Cambridge MA: Harvard University Press).

Wassermann, J. (1985), *Caspar Hauser* (New York: Carroll & Graf Publishers).

Wegner. D.M. (2002), *The Illusion of Conscious Will* (Cambridge MA: MIT Press).

Wilkinson, G.S. (1984), 'Reciprocal food sharing in the vampire bat', *Nature*, **308**, 181–4.

Wittgenstein, L. (1922), *Tractatus Logico-Philosophicus*, English translation by D F. Pears and B.F. McGuinness (London: Routledge and Kegan Paul).

Wittgenstein, L. (1953), *Philosophical Investigations*, English translation by G.E.M. Anscombe (Oxford: Blackwell).

Index